Illegal Immigration

Other Books of Related Interest:

Opposing Viewpoints Series

Domestic Terrorism

US Foreign Policy

Voting Rights

World Peace

At Issue Series

Does the World Hate the US?

Migrant Workers

Minorities and the Law

Should the US Close Its Borders?

Current Controversies Series

Gangs

Immigration

Politics and Religion

Racial Profiling

"Congress shall make no law . . . abridging the freedom of speech, or of the press."

First Amendment to the US Constitution

The basic foundation of our democracy is the First Amendment guarantee of freedom of expression. The Opposing Viewpoints series is dedicated to the concept of this basic freedom and the idea that it is more important to practice it than to enshrine it.

"Congress shall make
no law . . . abridging . . .
the freedom of speech,
or of the press."

First Amendment to the US Constitution

OPPOSING
VIEWPOINTS®
SERIES

Illegal Immigration

Noël Merino, Book Editor

GREENHAVEN PRESS
A part of Gale, Cengage Learning

GALE
CENGAGE Learning®

Farmington Hills, Mich • San Francisco • New York • Waterville, Maine
Meriden, Conn • Mason, Ohio • Chicago

Patricia Coryell, *Vice President & Publisher, New Products & GVRL*
Douglas Dentino, *Manager, New Products*
Judy Galens, *Acquisitions Editor*

For more information, contact:
Greenhaven Press
27500 Drake Rd.
Farmington Hills, MI 48331-3535
Or you can visit our Internet site at gale.cengage.com

Articles in Greenhaven Press anthologies are often edited for length to meet page requirements. In addition, original titles of these works are changed to clearly present the main thesis and to explicitly indicate the author's opinion. Every effort is made to ensure that Greenhaven Press accurately reflects the original intent of the authors. Every effort has been made to trace the owners of copyrighted material.

Cover Image copyright © Patrick Poendl/Shutterstock.com.

LIBRARY OF CONGRESS CATALOGING-IN-PUBLICATION DATA

Illegal immigration / Noël Merino, book editor.
    pages cm. -- (Opposing viewpoints)
Summary: "Opposing Viewpoints is the leading source for libraries and classrooms in need of current-issue materials. The viewpoints are selected from a wide range of highly respected sources and publications"-- Provided by publisher.
    Includes bibliographical references and index.
    ISBN 978-0-7377-7272-2 (hardback) -- ISBN 978-0-7377-7273-9 (paperback)
1. Illegal aliens--United States--Juvenile literature. 2. United States--Emigration and immigration--Juvenile literature. I. Merino, Noël.
    JV6465.I449 2014
    325--dc23
                                                                        2014032838

Printed in the United States of America
1 2 3 4 5 6 7 19 18 17 16 15

Contents

Chapter 3: Are Illegal Immigrants Treated Justly?

Chapter 4: How Should US Immigration Policy Be Reformed?

Why Consider Opposing Viewpoints?

> *"The only way in which a human being can make some approach to knowing the whole of a subject is by hearing what can be said about it by persons of every variety of opinion and studying all modes in which it can be looked at by every character of mind. No wise man ever acquired his wisdom in any mode but this."*
>
> John Stuart Mill

In our media-intensive culture it is not difficult to find differing opinions. Thousands of newspapers and magazines and dozens of radio and television talk shows resound with differing points of view. The difficulty lies in deciding which opinion to agree with and which "experts" seem the most credible. The more inundated we become with differing opinions and claims, the more essential it is to hone critical reading and thinking skills to evaluate these ideas. Opposing Viewpoints books address this problem directly by presenting stimulating debates that can be used to enhance and teach these skills. The varied opinions contained in each book examine many different aspects of a single issue. While examining these conveniently edited opposing views, readers can develop critical thinking skills such as the ability to compare and contrast authors' credibility, facts, argumentation styles, use of persuasive techniques, and other stylistic tools. In short, the Opposing Viewpoints Series is an ideal way to attain the higher-level thinking and reading skills so essential in a culture of diverse and contradictory opinions.

In addition to providing a tool for critical thinking, Opposing Viewpoints books challenge readers to question their own strongly held opinions and assumptions. Most people form their opinions on the basis of upbringing, peer pressure, and personal, cultural, or professional bias. By reading carefully balanced opposing views, readers must directly confront new ideas as well as the opinions of those with whom they disagree. This is not to argue simplistically that everyone who reads opposing views will—or should—change his or her opinion. Instead, the series enhances readers' understanding of their own views by encouraging confrontation with opposing ideas. Careful examination of others' views can lead to the readers' understanding of the logical inconsistencies in their own opinions, perspective on why they hold an opinion, and the consideration of the possibility that their opinion requires further evaluation.

Evaluating Other Opinions

To ensure that this type of examination occurs, Opposing Viewpoints books present all types of opinions. Prominent spokespeople on different sides of each issue as well as well-known professionals from many disciplines challenge the reader. An additional goal of the series is to provide a forum for other, less known, or even unpopular viewpoints. The opinion of an ordinary person who has had to make the decision to cut off life support from a terminally ill relative, for example, may be just as valuable and provide just as much insight as a medical ethicist's professional opinion. The editors have two additional purposes in including these less known views. One, the editors encourage readers to respect others' opinions—even when not enhanced by professional credibility. It is only by reading or listening to and objectively evaluating others' ideas that one can determine whether they are worthy of consideration. Two, the inclusion of such viewpoints encourages the important critical thinking skill of objectively evaluating an author's credentials and bias. This evaluation will illuminate an author's reasons for taking a particular stance on an issue and will aid in readers' evaluation of the author's ideas.

It is our hope that these books will give readers a deeper understanding of the issues debated and an appreciation of the complexity of even seemingly simple issues when good and honest people disagree. This awareness is particularly important in a democratic society such as ours in which people enter into public debate to determine the common good. Those with whom one disagrees should not be regarded as enemies but rather as people whose views deserve careful examination and may shed light on one's own.

Thomas Jefferson once said that "difference of opinion leads to inquiry, and inquiry to truth." Jefferson, a broadly educated man, argued that "if a nation expects to be ignorant and free . . . it expects what never was and never will be." As individuals and as a nation, it is imperative that we consider the opinions of others and examine them with skill and discernment. The Opposing Viewpoints series is intended to help readers achieve this goal.

David L. Bender and Bruno Leone,
Founders

Introduction

"The sharp decline in the US population of unauthorized immigrants that accompanied the 2007–2009 recession has bottomed out, and the number may be rising again."

—Jeffrey S. Passel,
D'Vera Cohn, and
Ana Gonzalez-Barrera,
Pew Research Center

Illegal immigration in the United States continues to be an issue of controversy, with 11.7 million unauthorized immigrants estimated to be living in the United States in 2012, according to a 2013 report by the Pew Research Center. The center estimates that the number of illegal, or unauthorized, immigrants living in the United States has fallen in recent years from the 2007 height of 12.2 million. The research from 2012 found that 60 percent of unauthorized immigrants, or 7 million, live in just six states: California, Florida, Illinois, New Jersey, New York, and Texas. Approximately 6 million unauthorized immigrants from Mexico make up the majority of this population, accounting for 52 percent of the total illegal immigrant population.

Unauthorized, or illegal, immigrants are foreign-born noncitizens who do not have the legal status to be living in the United States. For many unauthorized immigrants, entrance to the United States is first granted legally through a work visa or a visitor visa, but after the visa expires the individual fails to leave the country, taking up residence illegally. For other unauthorized immigrants, they arrive by crossing the US border illegally, without a work or visitor visa. In each of these two manners, a law is broken either by failing to respect the terms of a visa or by failing to gain legal entry.

Illegal immigrants can be contrasted with individuals who are born in the United States—and thereby granted US citizenship—and those who are legal immigrants. Legal immigrants can have a legal status by being granted permanent residence, being admitted as a refugee, or having authorized temporary residence for work or as a family member of an authorized worker. Legal immigrants who become US citizens are noted as naturalized citizens.

Throughout this volume, various authors use different terminology to refer to unauthorized immigrants. In 2013 the Associated Press announced it would eliminate the use of "illegal immigrant" entirely, but many media outlets—including the *New York Times*—continue to use the terminology. Following the latter, the terminology is used in this volume interchangeably with "unauthorized immigrant." There is no terminology for which there are not detractors, and this terminology used here is intended to be neutral. The authors of the viewpoints vary in their use of terminology depending on their position on the issue, ranging from using the term "illegal" as a noun, to the use of "illegal alien," to the use of "undocumented worker." The term "illegal immigrant" as used here in the introduction and throughout is meant to be merely descriptive and without bias on the issue.

There is wide disagreement about what should be done about illegal immigrants already in the United States, not to mention the disagreement about policies governing immigration in the future. There is the question of what to do about the existing unauthorized immigrants, as well as the question of what to do about future prospective immigrants. The positions taken on the issue run the gamut. The Federation for American Immigration Reform (FAIR) believes that illegal immigration should not be rewarded by amnesty and citizenship, and that existing laws must be enforced to stop people from overstaying visas and from illegally entering the country. The National Immigration Forum advocates amnesty for existing unauthorized immigrants who meet certain criteria, with a path to citizenship, and it also advocates humane enforcement of existing laws. Yet, some libertarian groups argue that the concept of borders should be abandoned, allowing the free movement of people without concern of citizenship or other legal status.

The issue of illegal immigration in the United States has long been a source of controversy and continues to be so today. In *Opposing Viewpoints: Illegal Immigration*, authors take a variety of viewpoints on the subject of illegal immigration in chapters titled "How Does Illegal Immigration Impact the United States?," "How Effective Are Policies to Stop Illegal Immigration?," "Are Illegal Immigrants Treated Justly?," and "How Should US Immigration Policy Be Reformed?" The divergent viewpoints of this volume illustrate that there is wide disagreement about the extent to which illegal immigration is a problem and how best to deal with it.

CHAPTER 1

How Does Illegal Immigration Impact the United States?

Chapter Preface

The Pew Research Center estimates that out of more than eleven million unauthorized immigrants living in the United States in 2010, eight million were in the nation's workforce. This means that unauthorized immigrant workers in 2010 made up 5.2 percent of the labor force, while being only 3.7 percent of the nation's population. The states with the largest share of unauthorized immigrants—Nevada, California, Texas, and New Jersey—also have a high percentage of unauthorized immigrant workers in the workforce. Nevada has the highest percentage, with unauthorized immigrants accounting for one in ten workers. California has approximately 1.85 million unauthorized immigrants in the workforce, the largest number of unauthorized workers in any state in the country.

There are many concerns about the impact of illegal immigration on employment that come from all sides of the immigration debate. Concerns range from how unauthorized immigrants in the workforce affect legal immigrants and Americans, as well as how this illegal work affects the unauthorized workers themselves. The Federation for American Immigration Reform (FAIR) argues that illegal immigrant workers have a negative effect on the employment conditions in certain sectors. As FAIR explains, "The willingness of foreign workers to accept lower wages because of their illegal status acts to depress wages and working conditions for all workers in that occupation. This in turn makes employment in that sector less attractive to US workers who have other options." This, FAIR argues, is why people think that immigrants take jobs no American would take, but in fact this perception is shaped by illegal immigration itself. The employment organization Workplace Fairness argues that abuse of unauthorized immigrant workers is a problem. It states, "Undocumented workers are among the most vulnerable and exploited workers in our country, as frequent victims of unpaid wages, dangerous conditions and uncompensated workplace injuries, discrimination, and other labor law violations. Workers who attempt to remedy the abuse routinely face physical and immigration-related threats and retaliation."

Not all commentary on the impact of illegal immigration on US employment is negative, however. David Bier of the Competitive Enterprise Institute argues that the presence of low-skilled immigrants, whether legal or illegal, benefits the economy and raises American wages.

There is no doubt that illegal immigration has an impact on the United States. As the authors of the viewpoints in this chapter illustrate, however, there is wide disagreement about what that impact is and whether it is positive or negative for the United States.

> "What we have is a de facto quasi-guest-
> worker system."

There's No Such Thing as an Illegal Immigrant

Eric Posner

In the following viewpoint, Eric Posner argues that the reality of illegal immigration in the United States is that there exists, in reality, a "quasi-guest-worker" program. Posner claims that laws against illegal immigration are barely enforced, as the current system with high levels of illegal immigration serves the interests of the United States. He concludes that an official guest-worker program should replace the current system. Posner is Kirkland and Ellis Distinguished Service Professor of Law at the University of Chicago Law School.

As you read, consider the following questions:

1. What are the three tiers of the US immigration system, according to Posner?

2. Posner contends that the United States has an appetite for unskilled labor, citing what six jobs as examples?

3. According to the author, the real obstacle to developing an official guest-worker program is that such a program could solve illegal immigration only under what conditions?

An estimated 11 million people live in the United States illegally. Everyone agrees that this is intolerable, and—deportation being impossible and possibly unfair—Congress appears on the verge of granting them a path to citizenship. But legal reform is not going to solve the problem of illegal immigration. That's because illegal immigration is not really a problem, or if it is a problem, it is a problem that no one wants to solve.

The Reality of Illegal Immigration

It is common to think that the huge pool of illegal immigrants reflects a failure of government. Congress has established rules that determine who gets in and who stays out, but has failed to spend the money to enforce the law. The solution is more enforcement resources, symbolized by the huge wall being constructed among the Saguaros [cacti that grow in the desert of the American Southwest] in the Sonoran Desert.

But the reality is that the United States has long been well served by a three-tiered system of immigration. The top tier consists of highly desired foreign workers, who are offered green cards, which typically lead to citizenship. The second tier consists of skilled and semiskilled people who can obtain short-term visas, usually for three years. Some of them prove themselves while here and end up acquiring a green card as well. Then there is a third tier, typically unskilled people, who can be removed at any time and for any reason, yet are frequently permitted certain privileges, such as a driver's license. They are also permitted to work—while in practice being denied the protection of employment and labor laws. We call these people "illegal immigrants" but that is a misnomer. Little effort is made to stop them from working or to expel them. And those who proved themselves by staying employed, learning English, and making enough money to afford a moderate fine, were given a path to citizenship in 1986, as may occur again if Congress passes immigration reform this year [2013].

Illegal immigrants do break the law, but they break the law in the sense that everyone breaks the law. Think of traffic laws, which everyone breaks but which are also only enforced selectively—largely against people suspected of committing drug crimes or other misdeeds. The law against illegal entry is (sort of) enforced at the border, but hardly at all against people once they arrive, except if they commit serious crimes, in which case they are sent to jail and then deported.

It is an open secret that illegal workers are, or have been, employed by some of the country's largest and most important companies, like Tyson Foods. Yet the number of work site enforcement actions—where federal immigration authorities raid a work site and drag away illegal workers—has been minuscule. In 2011, work site raids resulted in the arrest of 1,471 illegal workers out of an estimated 8 million. In the same year, only 385 employers out of 6 million were fined for hiring illegal workers. And this counted for an increase from 2006, when precisely zero employers were punished. In other words, the odds of being punished for participating in the illegal immigration economy are something like the odds of being given a ticket for driving 56 mph in a 55 mph zone. Despite the federal system E-Verify, efforts to force employers to check the status of job applicants have mostly foundered because of their cost and the risk that lawful residents will be mistakenly deemed illegal (though this is in fact rare). Which is just to say that we are unwilling to incur the enforcement costs because we don't actually want to enforce.

A System Serving America's Interests

What we have is a de facto quasi-guest-worker system, where foreign workers who overstay their visas or sneak across the

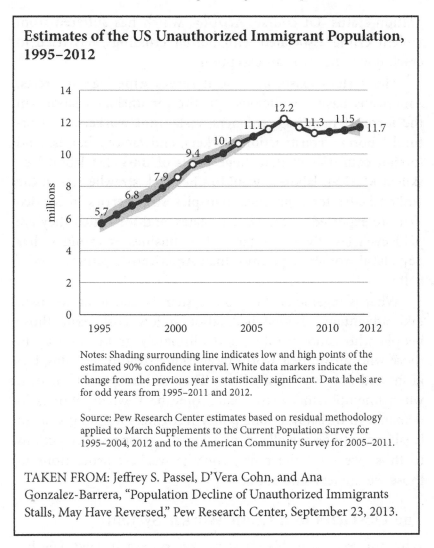

Estimates of the US Unauthorized Immigrant Population, 1995–2012

Notes: Shading surrounding line indicates low and high points of the estimated 90% confidence interval. White data markers indicate the change from the previous year is statistically significant. Data labels are for odd years from 1995–2011 and 2012.

Source: Pew Research Center estimates based on residual methodology applied to March Supplements to the Current Population Survey for 1995–2004, 2012 and to the American Community Survey for 2005–2011.

TAKEN FROM: Jeffrey S. Passel, D'Vera Cohn, and Ana Gonzalez-Barrera, "Population Decline of Unauthorized Immigrants Stalls, May Have Reversed," Pew Research Center, September 23, 2013.

border are permitted to stay and work as long as they do not commit a serious crime, look like terrorists, or cause other trouble. In many places, authorities take pains to assure illegal immigrants that they will not be turned over to federal [U.S.] Immigration and Customs Enforcement so that they will co-operate with the police and social services. Anxious to attract new residents, Baltimore, for example, prohibits its employees, including police, from asking anyone about his or her immigration status. Of course, Arizona, which has suffered from violent crime associated with border crossings, has tried to crack down, but it is an exception.

The system exists because it serves America's interests. Americans have a voracious appetite for unskilled labor—in the form of nannies, gardeners, restaurant workers, agricultural laborers, construction workers, and factory hands. And foreign countries contain huge pools of unskilled labor. Unskilled Mexican laborers would rather pick strawberries in the United States for a pittance than pick strawberries in Mexico that are exported to the United States, and for which they are paid even less than a pittance. U.S. businesses would rather pay illegal workers a pittance than Americans a pittance and a half.

What is ingenious about our system is that it allows us to take advantage of unskilled labor at low cost; exile those people who cause trouble; and ultimately grant amnesty to those who prove their worth by working steadily, learning English, and obeying criminal law. They will leave on their own when unemployment rises, and come back when labor is in demand. In this way, public policy recognizes a sliding scale of legal protections for aliens, offering the strongest protections to those we want the most, and the weakest protections to those we are less sure about.

The Obstacles to a Guest-Worker System

Why not recognize this guest-worker system in law? The bipartisan framework for immigration reform hints at such a change without explicitly endorsing it. But others have proposed this, and it was seriously considered in 2007 immigration reform negotiations.

The idea of making our guest-worker system official is to move potential illegal workers into legal channels, where they can be tracked and also protected from exploitation. Liberals have long opposed any system that creates second-class citizens, but because liberals also oppose harsh immigration enforcement measures, they end up reaping the benefits of a pool of low-wage second-class citizens without calling them that. Unions oppose guest-worker programs because union organization requires a long-term commitment, which temporary workers cannot make, while they compete with union members for jobs.

But these are not the real obstacles to a guest-worker program. Enshrined in law, such a system could solve the problem of illegal immigration only if it authorized the same low wages and bad working conditions that illegal workers currently accept. The demand for such workers is so high precisely because they lack legal protections and can be paid little and often treated poorly. The more generous the guest-worker program is, the more likely that it will be evaded. At the same time, however, neither Republicans nor Democrats will support a guest-worker program that permits foreign workers to be paid less than the minimum wage. And guest workers, like illegal immigrants, integrate themselves here and have children who become American citizens. It would be difficult to demand or force them to leave if they do not want to. In the end, they are not really guests.

Here's a prediction. A path to citizenship will be offered to the current 11 million, and if it is not too onerous, most of them will take it. But others will not, planting the seeds of a new illegal population. Possibly a guest-worker program will be put into place, but even if so, it will be too small and too entangled with bureaucracy for employers and workers to want to use. Over the years, millions more people from Mexico and especially (as Mexico's economy continues to improve) Central and South America will illegally enter the United States. They will be partly drawn by jobs, and partly by waiting family and friends, and the law will not deter them because they expect that sooner or later another path to citizenship will open up. Ten or 20 years from now, everyone will recognize a new illegal immigration "problem," which we will again "solve" by removing the "illegal" label from the foreheads of the migrants and affixing the "legal" label in its place.

> *"Illegal immigration goes on because . . . it serves the interest . . . of tens of millions of people."*

Illegal Immigration: Who Benefits?

Victor Davis Hanson

In the following viewpoint, Victor Davis Hanson argues that the reason there are millions of illegal immigrants residing in the United States is due to the special interest groups that benefit from their presence, including the nation of Mexico, employers in certain industries, the elite, and the Democratic Party. He argues that the solution is to close the border and ignore special interest groups that desire the status quo. Hanson is the Martin and Illie Anderson Senior Fellow at the Hoover Institution and chair of its military history working group.

As you read, consider the following questions:

1. According to the author, the amount of money sent back to Latin American countries each year by illegal immigrants might exceed how much?

2. Why does Hanson believe that illegal immigrants warp civic statistics about the upward mobility of Latinos?

3. At what point does Hanson think that illegal immigrants in the United States could start on a path to legal status?

Why are over 11 million foreign nationals residing illegally in the United States? If we can answer that question, then we can fathom the purpose of "comprehensive immigration reform," and understand why special-interest groups mostly favor what the majority of Americans oppose. Illegal immigration goes on because, in the Roman sense, it serves the interest (*cui bono?*) of tens of millions of people. In practical terms, "comprehensive immigration reform" is a way not to end the present chaos but to legitimize it.

Let us count the concerned beneficiaries.

1) Mexico. Someday Mexico, a nation rich in natural resources, may achieve rough parity with the other North American economies and develop truly consensual and transparent government. Someday the declining birth rate in Mexico may make Mexico City husband its suddenly precious manpower. Someday the Rio Grande may become as abstract as the border between the U.S. and Canada.

That someday, however, is not now. At present, Mexico views the United States as a safety valve for potential social unrest, seeing it in much the same way as Easterners once envisioned the American West—a place that the impoverished but audacious might flee to rather than agitate against vast inequality at home.

No one knows how many billions of dollars illegal aliens annually send back to Mexico and other Latin American countries, but the figure may exceed $30 billion—a source of foreign exchange as valuable as oil exports or tourism. That Mexico's own citizens residing in the United States often live in poverty in order to budget for their weekly remittances, or that U.S. taxpayers subsidize such beneficence through entitlements, is of little, if any, concern to Mexico City.

Finally, the export of millions of Mexican nationals gives Mexico City political leverage with the United States, whether exercised through the ubiquity of Mexican consulates here, the constant sermonizing about the plight of the dispossessed, or the surreal lawsuits against particular American states. For real reform to succeed, Mexico would have to resign itself to far fewer remittances, potentially greater social unrest, landmark social reform at home, and less traction with the American government. For those reasons alone, it will bitterly oppose real, rather than the present Potemkin, reform.

2) Business. Employers in the restaurant and hospitality industries, and in meat packing, agribusiness, construction, and landscaping, find Mexican nationals wonderful workers. They are. The lack of legality, English, and a high school diploma are not drawbacks for the physically demanding jobs in these fields, but in a tragically paradoxical way become advantages—turning what would otherwise be entry level or temporary employment into a multiyear ordeal. The employer reaps the benefit of industrious young and healthy workers, and the greater society picks up the eventual tab for the aging and injured and for dependents in terms of health care, education, and law enforcement costs.

In an economy of long-standing 7-plus percent unemployment, employers could surely find American workers, but not, by and large, workers as industrious as Mexican nationals, and not as low paid, since the assorted costs of the Mexican workers' achieving nominal parity with American citizens are borne by the society at large. Do not expect business to favor any reform that changes the advantageous status quo.

To be fair to employers, if our society wishes to close the border, then it must be prepared to pay higher prices for some commodities, at least in the short term, on the theory that, in terms of social stability and economic justice, training and employing American citizens might in the long run be less expensive than permitting the influx of illegal aliens to continue. Bottom line: Expect employers to resent bitterly true immigration reform that would halt the influx of cheap labor. In every "grand bargain," there will be a Republican shilling for big business.

3) The elite. Inexpensive foreign "household help"—gardeners, nannies, housekeepers, cooks—is now a fixture among the wealthy and upper-middle classes of the American Southwest, which are emulating the values and lifestyle of the 19th-century aristocracy. For many American suburban elites, illegal immigration is largely seen in personal terms as a patron-client relationship with particular immigrants. The Atherton or Newport investment banker or computer engineer sees himself as a concerned noble offering needed employment to an equally noble client—as a sort of American version of the *patrón* who assumes social obligations in addition to paying wages. In psychological terms, the member of the blue-state elite envisions himself not as an exploiter of cheap labor, but rather more as a benefactor of the greater social good. That the Burlingame Software executive would never hire an unemployed African-American youth to cut his lawn, given his preference for a Mexican landscape, is somehow seen as liberal.

Anecdotes (e.g., "I give all my extra clothes to Herlinda"; "We bought a used car for José"), not statistics, guide these people's thinking. In the elite mind, there is no contradiction between hiring Roberto to build a redwood fence in the backyard and ensuring that one's own kids go to private schools to avoid joining Roberto's kids in the neighborhood school in nearby Redwood City. Roberto is a wonderful handyman, but his children are not the sort of chums that Stanford-bound offspring should associate with or be forced to slow down with in an English class. Crass nativists and racists live in places like southern Arizona and Bakersfield; liberal apartheid

The National Council of La Raza (NCLR)

The National Council of La Raza (NCLR) has succeeded in defining, on its own terms, the parameters of the immigration debate by smearing critics of its agendas as "anti-immigrant" racists. Typical was a 2008 campaign called "We Can Stop the Hate." Launched by NCLR with the assistance of the Center for American Progress, Media Matters [for America], and the Mexican American Legal Defense and Educational Fund (MALDEF), this campaign was overtly designed to silence critics who raised alarms about mass illegal immigration into the United States, and who opposed amnesty and open borders. The . . . campaign portrayed such concerns as the "rhetoric of hate groups, nativists, and vigilantes."

"The Premise That America Is Racist, Hateful, and Discriminatory," Discoverthenetworks.org.

progressives, eager to ensure social justice, hire illegal aliens in places like Atherton to help the proverbial people. They use their ample income and capital to ensure a social apartness that avoids the realities that those without their disposable income deal with in a quite different fashion. Expect a suburban elite to oppose any true reform that would imperil their own psychological penance and clear material benefits.

4) La Raza. The presence of 11 million illegal aliens—largely from the poorer provinces of Mexico, the majority non-English-speaking and without high school educations—warps all civic statistics about the upward mobility of Latinos. Translated, that means a third-generation American of partial Mexican ancestry, with a Latinate last name but not speaking Spanish, qualifies as a minority for purposes of hiring and admissions. The apparent theory is that his cohort has not achieved statistical parity with the majority, ostensibly because of ongoing but rectifiable discrimination, rather than because of the continuing influx of newcomers from impoverished Oaxaca.

Why would ethnic elites in journalism, politics, academia, and public employment wish to alter the present advantageous nonsystem? Illegal immigration has turned much of the American Southwest into a blue political haven. What the *La Raza* elite fears is a collective ethnic trajectory analogous to the Italian-American experience, where Latinate tribal identification becomes incidental rather than essential to one's character, and where politics are predicated on issues rather than a quid-pro-quo patron-client bargain. Is there a *La Raza* that clamors for more immigration from bankrupt Sicily or seeks affirmative action for Italians tarred by slurs of affinity with *La Cosa Nostra*? Does any other identity group adopt the nomenclature "The Race"?

With the end of illegal immigration, in a generation or two the very word *La Raza* or Chicano would disappear from the American parlance, buried under the juggernaut of assimilation, intermarriage, and integration. Only the influx of millions of illegal aliens replenishes the unassimilated ethnic pool and thereby ensures through the ensuing disparities that the Latino caucus, the Chicano Studies Department, and the accented name of the evening newsreader do not go the way of Italian-, Armenian-, or Greek-American assimilation.

Under the present win-win scenario, expect the ethnic elite to oppose bitterly any true reform measure that would close the border and someday make "Hispanic" or "Latino" as significant as "German," "Romanian," or "Polish"—a rubric of occasional ethnic pride but without any measurable political clout.

5) The Democratic Party. If it was true that under the 1986 amnesty, less than half of the concerned foreign nationals chose to become citizens, that would not be the case with an updated version. Much has changed politically in the last 30 years. We can disagree over the reasons why "Latino" has become synonymous with "Democratic," but not over the political results. The Left cites conservative insensitivity to the plight of the Latin American poor; the Right points to cynical political manipulation that offers assorted entitlements in exchange for ethnic loyalty manifested by second-generation voters and a sense of solidarity that permeates American citizens of Latin American ancestry. No matter—any amnesty this time around would see much greater participation rates to fuel ongoing political momentum.

In any Gang of Eight–style caucus, assume that its Democratic members would not wish to endanger the present political realities that have changed the electoral map of the southwestern United States. In cynical fashion, Democrats will grant concessions on guest workers to pacify Republican grandees fronting for business, in exchange for amnesties that will maintain demographic dividends and their own political futures. As a general rule of thumb, any time a Democratic legislator praises a Republican counterpart for being reasonable and sensitive, we can equate such magnanimity with private guffaws about the naïveté—if not greed—of his opposite number. How ironic that the "Latino" vote is probably not what lost the Republicans the last election—instead, it was the working-class whites who stayed home because they sensed that they were not a part of Mitt Romney's world, and who mostly oppose blanket amnesties unless they come with iron-clad assurances of closed borders.

And what about the American people? The public that feels most immediately the social costs of illegal immigration bitterly resents the cynical nonenforcement of the law. Whereas professors in Maine or Wisconsin may see a liberal civil rights issue, ranchers along the border or parents whose children are at a school in Tulare see only illiberality: the public bearing the social costs of employers' greed, and an ethnic lobby practicing a disturbing chauvinism concerned not with illegal immigration per se, but only with illegal immigration from Latin America. (Were 1 million Chinese arriving illegally each year, *La Raza* would be decrying nonenforcement of the law and unfair competition to American workers.)

In the same manner in which principled skepticism concerning gay marriage became homophobia, support for fracking made one a polluter, doubts about the government's responsibility to provide wealthy women with free birth control equated with misogyny, or worries over curbing the Second Amendment were synonymous with redneck heartlessness, so too border enforcement is now tantamount to nativism and racism—charges analogous to child molestation for most Americans today.

Solutions? Close the border. Deport illegal aliens who are not working and have been regularly on public assistance, have violated U.S. criminal laws, or have just recently arrived. *After* that, allow the law-abiding, employed long-term resident to pay a fine and remain on U.S. soil, while learning English and applying for citizenship—from the rear of the line. Aid the transition of American citizens off state support into the labor force; take the moral high ground with Mexico and demand respect for U.S. sovereignty and U.S. laws. Do not be bullied by *La Raza*, and instead understand the basis of its philological reality. Do not let yourself be demagogued by false charges of nativism and racism. Worry more about unemployed American citizens and stressed taxpayers than about Mexican nationals who are fleeing a nation rich in natural resources and in need of millions of reformers.

All that should be the basis for immigration reform—and thereby will ensure outrage from the special interests that are so heavily vested in the present violation of the law.

> "High unemployment is not only a re-
> sult of stressed market factors, but it
> has also been created—and pro-
> longed—by our illegal immigration
> problem."

Unemployment and Illegal Immigration

Bob Confer

*In the following viewpoint, Bob Confer argues that high unem-
ployment in the United States is partially caused by illegal immigrants who take jobs that Americans could do. Confer claims
that if all the jobs now taken by illegal immigrants were given to
unemployed Americans, the unemployment problem would be
solved. He contends that the only thing necessary to achieve this
goal is to enforce the existing immigration laws. Confer is an
opinion columnist at the* New American *magazine.*

As you read, consider the following questions:

1. According to Confer, approximately how many million
   Americans are without a job?

2. The author contends that if labor and immigration laws were enforced, it would create up to how many job openings?

3. Confer cites a source finding that how many million jobs held by illegal immigrants are skilled?

The biggest issue weighing on the minds of Americans is the economy. Recent decreases in factory orders and consumer confidence, coupled with unemployment/ underemployment nearing 16 percent, have many of those fortunate to have a job once again questioning their job security and financial well-being while those who cannot find a job fret over their long-term prospects after more than two years of economic malaise.

Another issue that remains at the forefront of any discussion concerning America's health is illegal immigration. Thanks to Arizona's much-needed and much-welcomed approach to self-preservation in the face of the federal government's failure to secure the border, our citizens debate on a daily basis what needs to be done to address this problem that has haunted us for decades and has, for the second time in the past 25 years, reached its tipping point.

Despite how these two issues dominate the political talk of the day and how different they seem, most people are oblivious to the fact that they are intertwined: High unemployment is not only a result of stressed market factors, but it has also been created—and prolonged—by our illegal immigration problem. Americans are unable to find gainful employment because jobs are being held by non-Americans who have illegally entered our borders unabated and are illegally employed by companies both large and small. The proof for this claim can be found in a simple breakdown of the numbers.

When looking at the details behind the Department of Labor's June [2010] jobs report it can be concluded that there were a total of 17.2 million Americans without a job, that gi-

Estimate of Illegal Immigrants	
Illegal aliens in country	25,360,894
Other than Mexican (OTM) in country	670,216

TAKEN FROM: ImmigrationCounters.com, accessed June 12, 2014.

gantic sum including those identified as "unemployed" by the government as well as those considered to be "marginally attached" to the workforce.

In his July 1 speech about immigration—his first regarding this matter while in office—President Barack Obama said there were 11 million undocumented immigrants in the United States, numbers comparable to Department of Homeland Security estimations. We know this value is likely very low, as many sources on both sides of the issue (those for open borders, those for regulated borders) peg the number of illegal aliens closer to 20 million. ImmigrationCounters.com— which compiles its statistics using data from numerous public and private sources—puts the population at just under 23 million.

A 2006 report by Catholic Online analyzed the demographics of these transients and noted that 37.5 percent of the then estimated 12 million illegal immigrants were children, meaning 62.5 percent were adults. If those percentages are accurate to this day, which they likely are, that equates to 14.4 million adult aliens.

Now, consider what brings the illegals to America. It's the same thing that brought—and brings—countless legal immigrants to our land: jobs. Thanks to opportunity and a quality of life that is unmatched on this planet (a result of the principles of liberty and free markets in action), the USA has become a destination for Latino job seekers who want to stake a claim and better their lives here or send money back home to Mexico and Central American countries to support their kin.

That importance for the dollar and the workers' assumption of support for their extended families abroad (not to mention the reward for the risk taken to cross the border and live freely in a land in which they don't belong) probably means that most of the adult illegal immigrants are working within our borders.

If labor and immigration laws were enforced—and amnesty not granted as the Washington establishment would prefer—that would create up to 14.4 million job openings, satisfying a good many of the 17.2 million jobless legal residents of this nation. That would result in an unemployed population as low as 2.8 million Americans, which works out to be an unemployment rate of 1.8 percent, an absurdly low number far below what many economists consider full employment (four to five percent).

Many supporters of amnesty and unchecked immigration will say that such an assumption is unrealistic because the illegals are supposedly doing jobs that Americans won't do. That exaggeration is grossly incorrect for two reasons: One, statistics show otherwise and, two, Americans will work if given the chance. According to ImmigrationCounters.com, the aliens aren't doing only the most menial of chores; 11.7 million of their jobs held are skilled positions (construction, maintenance, and the like). Regarding the remaining jobs (those of the low-skill sort), they would become utilized by the American worker were unemployment insurance to actually follow its predetermined allotments and not be extended at every chance possible by Congress (which forces dependency on government). The unemployed would chose to take the career path (if only temporarily) that they had not previously considered.

It is obvious that in order to straighten out the economy and get more Americans working, government at all levels—local, state, and federal—must focus on the enforcement of existing laws and responsibilities and address the immigration problem in a timely, legal, and effective manner. There's no need to reinvent the wheel and create new legislation because good laws are already there. They're just not being enforced. If state agencies came down hard on the companies that employ illegals and the federal government followed its constitutional obligation to protect the states from invasion, our nation and its economy would get a much-needed boost.

| "There is simply no evidence that immigration drives up the U.S. unemployment rate or that it drives down wages for American workers."

There Is No Evidence That Illegal Immigrants Take Jobs from Americans

Daniel Griswold

In the following viewpoint, Daniel Griswold argues that although many have blamed high US unemployment on illegal immigration, data show the opposite. Griswold claims that most immigrants do not compete for jobs with US-born citizens and that immigration generally boosts the wages of Americans. Griswold contends that the best tool for economic recovery would be to increase the channels for immigrants to legally enter and work in the United States. Griswold is president of the National Association of Foreign-Trade Zones.

As you read, consider the following questions:

1. According to the author, how many more illegal immigrants were in the United States four years ago when the unemployment rate was 5 percent?

2. Griswold contends that immigration boosts the wages of all American employees except for what class of workers?

3. According to the author, how many workers are there in the United States?

Recent hearings [2011] in the Republican-controlled House judiciary subcommittee on immigration focused on enforcement, but the underlying message was that immigrants are taking jobs that rightfully belong to American workers.

The U.S. Unemployment Rate

The implication was clear: If we can reduce illegal immigration, it will mean more jobs and higher wages for native-born workers, especially the poor and minorities.

That message may play well politically, but it does not reflect the reality of America's dynamic labor market. There is simply no evidence that immigration drives up the U.S. unemployment rate or that it drives down wages for American workers.

America's current unemployment rate of nearly 9 percent has nothing to do with immigration. The rate was below 5 percent four years ago when, according to the Pew Hispanic Center, there were 1 million *more* illegal immigrants in the United States than today.

In fact, immigration helps to soften swings in the unemployment rate by acting as a kind of safety valve for the U.S. labor market. When jobs are plentiful and labor markets tight, immigrants tend to come in greater numbers. When jobs are

Economic and Demographic Realities Drive Immigration

According to recent projections by the U.S. Department of Labor, hundreds of thousands of net new jobs will be created during the next decade for home health aides, food preparation and serving workers, retail salespersons, landscaping and groundskeeping workers, and waiters and waitresses.

At the same time, the number of Americans who have traditionally filled such jobs continues to shrink. American workers, on average, are becoming older and better educated and thus less willing to fill those jobs. The number of adult Americans in the workforce without a high school diploma has dropped by 3 million in the past decade, and that trend will likely continue. . . .

Immigrants fill the growing gap between expanding low-skilled jobs and the shrinking pool of native-born Americans who would want such jobs. Immigrant workers enable important sectors of the U.S. economy to continue to grow and meet the needs of their customers.

Daniel Griswold, Testimony before the Subcommittee on Immigration and Border Security, Committee on the Judiciary, US House of Representatives, January 26, 2011.

scarce and unemployment high, immigrants arrive in fewer numbers and more choose to return to their native countries, an option not open to native-born Americans.

The Positive Impact of Immigration

The large majority of Americans have no reason to fear losing their job to an immigrant. Immigrants typically fill niches in the labor market at the high end and the low end of the skill spectrum, from farmworkers and dishwashers to computer scientists and physics professors. Of course, Americans perform those jobs as well, but not in sufficient numbers needed to meet demand during years of normal growth. As a result, immigrants complement most American workers rather than compete against them.

Numerous studies have found a generally positive impact of immigration on native-born wages. The only two groups that do suffer some wage losses because of immigration are other recent immigrants, and the small and shrinking pool of native-born adult Americans laboring without a high school diploma.

A comprehensive study by the National Research Council [NRC] in 1997 concluded that immigration boosts the income of American workers overall by as much as $10 billion, but that it does slightly reduce the wages of the lowest skilled Americans. The NRC found that immigration had no negative effect on the wages of black Americans as a group.

More recent studies have confirmed the benign impact of immigration on U.S. wages. In a 2006 study for the National Bureau of Economic Research, economists Gianmarco Ottaviano and Giovanni Peri estimated that immigration from 1990 to 2004 had reduced the wages of Americans without a high school diploma by 1 to 2 percent, while boosting the wages of the more than 90 percent of American adults with a high school education by 0.7 percent in the short run and 1.8 percent in the long run.

The Impact of Immigrant Workers

Immigrants have a relatively small impact on the wages of native-born workers for at least three major reasons.

One, immigrants tend to bring a different set of skills and differing preferences for the kind of work they perform compared to native-born workers, which means immigrants are less easily substituted for their native-born counterparts.

Two, by increasing the size of the labor force, immigrants tend to boost the returns to capital, stimulating more investment in the economy and thus raising the productivity and wages of all workers, including the native born.

Immigrants can also boost investment through their own human capital and entrepreneurial spirit. A 2007 Duke University study found that one-quarter of all engineering and technology companies launched between 1995 and 2005 had at least one key founder who was foreign born. Those companies with at least one immigrant cofounder produced $52 billion in sales and employed 450,000 workers in 2005.

Three, for all the political hype over immigration, the number of immigrants and their output continue to be modest compared to the overall size of a U.S. economy that employs close to 150 million workers and produces more than $14 trillion in output a year.

The best approach to immigration as our economy recovers from recession would be to expand channels for legal entry. Legal immigrants tend to invest more in their job and language skills, and they enjoy more bargaining power in the market place, resulting in higher wages not only for the immigrants but for Americans working alongside them.

There is a lot of blame to go around in Washington for the recession and the resulting loss of millions of jobs in the past few years. Immigrants working hard in our economy today are not part of the problem, but part of the solution.

| "*The problem . . . is that undocumented workers are not evenly distributed.*"

Do Illegal Immigrants Actually Hurt the U.S. Economy?

Adam Davidson

In the following viewpoint, Adam Davidson argues that there is generally a consensus that the overall economic impact of legal and illegal immigration is positive for the economy. However, Davidson claims that illegal immigration imposes costs that are usually concentrated in certain locales, thus creating a political barrier to resolving the issue through well-placed funding. Davidson is cofounder and cohost of NPR's Planet Money *and a weekly columnist for the* New York Times.

As you read, consider the following questions:

1. How many US adults lack a high school diploma, according to the author?

2. The author cites an expert who claims that undocumented workers contribute how much money to Social Security each year?

3. What areas of the country does the author cite as taking on substantial net costs due to undocumented immigrants?

Earlier this month [February 2013] I met Pedro Chan at his small apartment above an evangelical church in Brooklyn's Sunset Park neighborhood. Chan, who shares the place with three others, is short and muscular. He has a quiet voice and a patient demeanor that seems to have served him well on his journey to New York. In 2002, he left his Guatemalan village for a long trip through Mexico and, with the help of a smuggler, across the Texas border. In 2004, he made it to Brooklyn, where his uncle helped him find work on small construction crews.

These days, Chan helps skilled (and fully documented) carpenters, electricians and stucco installers do their jobs by carrying heavy things and cleaning the work site. For this, he earns up to $25,000 a year, which is considerably less than the average entry wage for New York City's 100,000 or so documented construction workers. Chan's boss, who spoke on the condition of anonymity, said that unless he learned a specialized skill, Chan would never be able to move up the income ladder. As long as there are thousands of undocumented workers competing for low-end jobs, salaries are more likely to fall than to rise.

The Impact of Illegal Immigration

As Congress debates the contours of immigration reform, many arguments have been made on economic grounds. Undocumented workers, some suggest, undercut wages and take jobs that would otherwise go to Americans. Worse, the argument goes, many use social programs, like hospitals and schools, that cost taxpayers and add to our $16 trillion national debt. Would deporting Pedro Chan and the other 11 million or so undocumented workers mean more jobs, lower taxes and a stronger economy?

Illegal immigration does have some undeniably negative economic effects. Similarly skilled native-born workers are faced with a choice of either accepting lower pay or not working in the field at all. Labor economists have concluded that undocumented workers have lowered the wages of U.S. adults without a high school diploma—25 million of them—by anywhere between 0.4 to 7.4 percent.

The impact on everyone else, though, is surprisingly positive. Giovanni Peri, an economist at the University of California, Davis, has written a series of influential papers comparing the labor markets in states with high immigration levels to those with low ones. He concluded that undocumented workers do not compete with skilled laborers—instead, they complement them. Economies, as Adam Smith argued in *The Wealth of Nations*, work best when workers become specialized and divide up tasks among themselves. Pedro Chan's ability to take care of routine tasks on a work site allows carpenters and electricians to focus on what they do best. In states with more undocumented immigrants, Peri said, skilled workers made more money and worked more hours; the economy's productivity grew. From 1990 to 2007, undocumented workers increased legal workers' pay in complementary jobs by up to 10 percent.

I saw this in action when Chan took me to his current work site, a two-story office building on Coney Island Avenue. The skilled workers had already installed wood flooring in a lawyer's office and were off to the next job site. That left Chan to clean up the debris and to install a new toilet. As I looked around, I could see how we were on one end of an economic chain reaction. Chan's boss no longer had to pay a highly skilled worker to perform basic tasks. That lowered the overall cost of construction, increasing the number of jobs the company could book, which meant more customers and more money. It reminded me of how so many restaurants operate. Without undocumented labor performing routine tasks, meals, which factor labor costs into the price, would be more expensive. There would also be fewer jobs for waiters and chefs.

The Economic Benefits

Earlier that day, I was reminded of another seldom-discussed fact about immigrant life in the United States. Immigrants spend most of the money they make. Chan had broken down his monthly expenses: $400 a month in rent, another $30 or so for gas, electric and Internet. He sends some money home and tries to save a few thousand a year in his Citibank account, but he ends up spending more than $10,000 annually. That includes the $1,400 or so he pays the I.R.S. [Internal Revenue Service] so that he can have a taxpayer I.D. number, which allows him to have a credit score so that he can rent an apartment or lease a car.

There are many ways to debate immigration, but when it comes to economics, there isn't much of a debate at all. Nearly all economists, of all political persuasions, agree that immigrants—those here legally or not—benefit the overall economy. "That is not controversial," Heidi Shierholz, an economist at the Economic Policy Institute, told me. Shierholz also said that "there is a consensus that, on average, the incomes of families in this country are increased by a small, but clearly positive amount, because of immigration."

The benefit multiplies over the long haul. As the baby boomers retire, the post-boom generation's burden to finance their retirement is greatly alleviated by undocumented immigrants. Stephen Goss, chief actuary for the Social Security Administration, told me that undocumented workers contribute about $15 billion a year to Social Security through payroll taxes. They only take out $1 billion (very few undocumented workers are eligible to receive benefits). Over the years, undocumented workers have contributed up to $300 billion, or nearly 10 percent, of the $2.7 trillion Social Security Trust Fund.

The Problem of Costs

The problem, though, is that undocumented workers are not evenly distributed. In areas like southern Texas and Arizona and even parts of Brooklyn, undocumented immigrants impose a substantial net cost to local and state governments, Shierholz says. Immigrants use public assistance, medical care and schools. Some immigrant neighborhoods have particularly high crime rates. Jared Bernstein, a fellow at the Center on Budget and Policy Priorities, told me that these are also areas in which low-educated workers are most likely to face stiff competition from immigrants. It's no wonder why so much political furor comes from these regions.

Undocumented workers represent a classic economic challenge with a fairly straightforward solution. Immigrants bring diffuse and hard-to-see benefits to average Americans while imposing more tangible costs on a few, Shierholz says. The dollar value of the benefits far outweigh the costs, so the government could just transfer extra funds to those local populations that need more help. One common proposal would grant amnesty to undocumented workers, which would create a sudden increase in tax payments. Simultaneously, the federal government could apply a percentage of those increased revenues to local governments.

But that, of course, seems politically improbable. Immigration is one of many problems—like another economic no-brainer: eliminating farm subsidies—in which broad economic benefits battle against a smaller, concentrated cost in one area. As immigration reform seems more likely than at any time in recent memory, it's important to remember that it is not the economic realities that have changed. It's the political ones.

"Criminal aliens—noncitizens who com-
mit crimes—are a growing threat to
public safety and national security, as
well as a drain on our scarce criminal
justice resources."

Illegal Immigrants Pose a Safety Threat and Drain Resources

Federation for American Immigration Reform (FAIR)

In the following viewpoint, the Federation for American Immigration Reform (FAIR) argues that illegal immigrants make up a disproportionately large percentage of prisoners, draining criminal justice resources at the federal and state levels. FAIR contends that certain states are especially burdened by illegal immigrant criminals. FAIR argues that illegal immigrants convicted of crimes should be deported from the United States. FAIR is a nonprofit organization that supports border security and lower immigration levels.

As you read, consider the following questions:

1. According to the author, how many illegal immigrants are in federal, state, and local prisons?

2. FAIR contends that its fiscal cost study in 2010 estimated that annual justice costs at the federal level related to illegal immigrants amounted to how much?

3. According to the author, what is notable about the percentage of illegal immigrant criminals in California and Arizona?

Criminal aliens—noncitizens who commit crimes—are a growing threat to public safety and national security, as well as a drain on our scarce criminal justice resources. In 1980, our federal and state prisons housed fewer than 9,000 criminal aliens. Today, about 55,000 criminal aliens account for more than one-fourth of prisoners in Federal Bureau of Prisons facilities, and there are about 297,000 criminal aliens incarcerated in state and local prisons. That number represents about 16.4 percent of the state and local prison population compared to the 12.9 percent of the total population comprised of foreign-born residents.

The Cost of Criminal Aliens

The estimated cost of incarcerating these criminal aliens at the federal level is estimated at $1.5 to $1.6 billion per year. That cost includes expenses in the federal prison system and the amount of money paid to state and local detention facilities in the State Criminal Alien Assistance Program (SCAAP). It does not include the costs of incarceration at the state and local level, nor does it include the related local costs of policing and the judicial system related to law enforcement against criminal aliens.

Our fiscal cost study in 2010 estimated administration of justice costs at the federal level related to criminal aliens at $7.8 billion annually. The comparable cost to state and local governments was $8.7 billion.

A Congressional Research Service report released in August 2012 found that over a 33-month period, between Octo-

Illegal Immigrants in Prison

State	Population	Estimated illegal immigrant population	Illegal immigrants as a percentage of the state population	Illegal immigrants as a percentage of the prison population
California	37,253,956	2,635,000	7.10%	12.70%
Texas	25,145,561	1,810,000	7.20%	5.50%
Florida	18,801,310	820,000	4.40%	5.10%
Illinois	12,830,632	550,000	4.30%	5.20%
North Carolina	9,535,483	410,000	4.30%	4.80%
New Jersey	8,791,894	410,000	4.70%	5.50%
Arizona	6,392,017	390,000	6.10%	11.70%
Oregon	3,831,074	170,000	4.40%	8.80%
Nevada	2,700,551	200,000	7.40%	8.50%
New Mexico	2,059,179	100,000	4.90%	5.40%

TAKEN FROM: Federation for American Immigration Reform (FAIR), "Criminal Aliens," 2012.

ber 2008 and July 2011, more than 159,000 illegal aliens were arrested by local authorities and identified by the federal government as deportable but nevertheless released back onto the streets. Nearly one-sixth of those same individuals were subsequently again arrested for crimes.

States with the Most Criminal Aliens

Using data collected in the SCAAP system for 2009, an average share of 5.4 percent of the prisoners in state and local prisons were criminal aliens. The share was more than double that average in California (12.7%) and Arizona (11.7%). Another seven states also had criminal alien shares higher than the national average. They were Oregon, Nevada, Colorado, Utah, New York, New Jersey, and Texas.

The shares of the incarcerated population comprised of criminal aliens are generally higher than the shares of the estimated illegal alien population in the state. For example, the estimated 2,365,000 illegal aliens in California represent 7.1 percent of the state's overall population compared to the 12.7 percent criminal alien population. Nationally, the estimated 11,920,000 illegal aliens in 2010 represented 3.9 percent of the overall population compared to the 5.4 percent criminal alien incarceration rate. This difference in shares demonstrates that the share of aliens in prison for various crimes is disproportionately large. The share of aliens in federal prisons is higher than in state and local prisons because federal prisons house aliens convicted of federal immigration offenses such as alien smuggling in addition to other crimes.

Ten states that accounted for 41 percent of the nation's total population in 2010 accounted for 63 percent of the nation's total population. Of those same states, all but Texas also have a share of the prison population that is larger than the estimated share of their illegal alien population.

Four Proposed Reforms

1. We must secure our borders. Denying jobs to illegal aliens through a centralized secure identity verification system is important to that effort.

2. We must assure that the criminal conviction of an alien leads to deportation and permanent exclusion from the United States.

3. Asylum applicants should be screened expeditiously and excluded if their claims are not credible. Even if they appear to have credible claims, they should be detained until background checks are done.

4. Other corrective measures include greater federal and local government cooperation to identify criminal aliens. The expansion of the Secure Communities program is useful in that regard, but it is no substitute for the 287(g) program that trains and deputizes local law enforcement personnel in immigration law enforcement.

| *"As the illegal immigrant population has grown, crime has, well, gone south."*

Illegal Immigrants Do Not Pose a Safety Threat

Steve Chapman

In the following viewpoint, Steve Chapman argues that despite well-publicized fears to the contrary, a rise in illegal immigration in the United States has not led to a rise in crime. Chapman contends that the continued inflow of illegal immigrants in recent decades has coincided with a drop in crime. Chapman claims that despite the fact that illegal immigrants do break the law in coming to the United States, all evidence supports the view that once they arrive they are extremely law-abiding. Chapman is a columnist and editorial writer for the Chicago Tribune.

As you read, consider the following questions:

1. What percentage of Chicago's residents are Latino, according to Chapman?

2. The author cites a sociologist who claims that felonious behavior is less common among Mexican Americans than among what other racial group?

3. What fraction of the Los Angeles population is Hispanic, according to Chapman?

From listening to the more vigorous critics of illegal immigration, our porous borders are a grave threat to safety. Not only can foreign terrorists sneak in to target us, but the most vicious criminals are free to walk in and inflict their worst on innocent Americans.

The Fear of Illegal Immigrants

In xenophobic circles, this prospect induces stark terror. Fox News' Glenn Beck has decried an "illegal immigrant crime wave." A contributor to Patrick Buchanan's website asserts, "Every day, in the United States, thousands of illegal aliens unleash a reign of terror on Americans."

Sure they do. And I'm Penélope Cruz.

There is a surface logic here. If people are willing to commit the crime of slipping into the country without permission, it might stand to reason that they have no respect for our laws and will break even more once they're here. Add in Mexican drug lords and Central American gangs, and it looks like we should all be fleeing to Canada to save our hides.

Chicago's Latino residents have risen to 28 percent of the population, and among that population are many people who came illegally. So why doesn't it feel like we're fighting the battle of the Alamo?

Simple: The things that would happen if the alarmists were right simply have not happened. A continuing inflow of violent, predatory Latinos would produce an unprecedented epidemic of larceny and slaughter. In reality, as the illegal immigrant population has grown, crime has, well, gone south.

The Decline in Crime

Since 1986, the year of the infamous amnesty for illegal immigrants, the U.S. murder rate has plunged by 37 percent. (In Chicago, the number of homicides went from 747 in 1986 to 460 last year [in 2009].) Forcible rape is down 23 percent. Drunk driving fatalities are off by more than half. You are safer today than you were before all those undocumented interlopers arrived.

Much is made of the alleged fact that 30 percent of federal prison inmates are illegal immigrants. Actually, according to the Bureau of Justice Statistics, the correct figure is 14 percent, and many are in just for violating immigration laws. In prisons at the state level, where most violent crime is prosecuted, illegal immigrants account for less than 5 percent of all inmates.

How can all this be? It's partly because native-born Americans are less prone to senseless mayhem than they used to be. But it's also because people who come here from other countries are actually more law-abiding than the norm.

A 2007 report by the Immigration Policy Center noted that "for every ethnic group, without exception, incarceration rates among young men are lowest for immigrants, even those who are the least educated. This holds true especially for the Mexicans, Salvadorans and Guatemalans who make up the bulk of the undocumented population."

Harvard sociologist Robert Sampson, who has focused his research on Chicago neighborhoods, documents that felonious behavior is less common among Mexican-Americans, who constitute the biggest share of Latinos, than among whites. Second and third generation Latinos, contrary to what you might expect, fall into more crime than immigrants. But Sampson says that overall, "Mexican-American rates of violence are very similar to whites."

The Motivation of Immigrants

The phenomenon is so evident that it was even recognized in a recent article in the *American Conservative*—a magazine founded by the lusty nativist ("we're gonna lose our country") Patrick Buchanan. It was written by Ron Unz, who made some enemies among Latinos by pushing a California ballot initiative to sharply limit bilingual education in public schools, but who knows better than to regard Latinos as the enemy.

Unz points out that in the five most heavily Hispanic cities in the country, violent crime is "10 percent below the national urban average and the homicide rate 40 percent lower." In Los Angeles, which is half Hispanic and easily accessible to those sneaking over the southern border, the murder rate has plummeted to levels unseen since the tranquil years of the early 1960s.

This is not really hard to understand. Today, as ever, most foreigners who make the sacrifice of leaving home and starting over in a strange land do so not to mug grandmothers or molest children, but to find work that will give them a better life. Coming here illegally does not alter that basic motivation.

In other words, they want to become full-fledged Americans, and they're succeeding. Is there something scary about that?

Periodical and Internet Sources Bibliography

The following articles have been selected to supplement the diverse views presented in this chapter.

Edward Alden	"Immigration and Border Control," *Cato Journal*, vol. 32, no. 1, Winter 2012.
Michael Barone	"Shrinking Problem: Illegal Immigration from Mexico," *Washington Examiner*, April 24, 2012.
Steven A. Camarota and Karen Zeigler	"Are There Really Jobs Americans Won't Do?," Center for Immigration Studies, May 2013.
Arian Campo-Flores	"Why Americans Think Immigration Hurts the Economy," *Newsweek*, May 13, 2010.
Selwyn Duke	"Illegal Aliens Get More Welfare Benefits than Citizens," *New American*, April 8, 2011.
R. Cort Kirkwood	"Illegal Aliens: Economic Consequences," *New American*, November 10, 2010.
Peter Kirsanow and Carissa Mulder	"Illegal Immigration and Black Unemployment," *National Review Online*, February 18, 2013.
Christopher Matthews	"The Economics of Immigration: Who Wins, Who Loses and Why," *Time*, January 30, 2013.
Jason Richwine	"A Population Portrait: Who Illegal Immigrants Are, and What They Bring with Them," *National Review Online*, June 7, 2010.
Ray Walser, Jena Baker McNeill, and Jessica Zuckerman	"The Human Tragedy of Illegal Immigration: Greater Efforts Needed to Combat Smuggling and Violence," Heritage Foundation, *Backgrounder*, no. 2568, June 22, 2011.
Darrell M. West	"Seven Myths That Cloud Immigration Debate," *USA Today*, September 1, 2010.

How Effective Are Policies to Stop Illegal Immigration?

Chapter Preface

There are several policies in place in the United States to control illegal immigration. The Department of Homeland Security (DHS) manages border enforcement. One of the components of the Immigration Reform and Control Act of 1986 was increased funding for border security. Since then, appropriations for the US Border Patrol (USBP) have grown from less than $500,000,000 per year in 1993 to over $3,500,000,000 in 2013, about a third of the annual budget for the US Customs and Border Protection, the largest federal law enforcement agency within DHS. At the start of 2013, USBP had more than twenty thousand agents, with the vast majority posted at the southwest border. In addition, as of January 15, 2013, DHS had installed 352 miles of primary pedestrian fencing and 299 miles of vehicle fencing (for a total of 651 miles), as well as 36 miles of secondary fencing. USBP also uses surveillance to patrol the border.

According to data collected by USBP, apprehensions of deportable individuals at the border rose to a height of approximately 1,600,000 in 1986, fell in the next few years only to rise again to near that level in 2000. By 2012, there were fewer than 400,000 apprehensions of deportable individuals at the border. Despite these apprehensions, the USBP reports that the recidivism rate is high, with 17 percent of offenders getting caught at the border more than once in the year.

Border control to apprehend those who lack permission to enter the United States is but one component of border enforcement. After all, a large percentage of individuals who end up as unauthorized residents entered the United States on a valid work visa or traveler visa. The Congressional Research Service estimates that in 2013 alone there were 362 million travelers entering the United States, among which 205,000 were denied admission. Among those who travel to the United

States, the Visa Waiver Program allows nationals from certain countries to enter the United States as temporary visitors for business or pleasure without obtaining a visa.

US Immigration and Customs Enforcement (ICE), with an annual budget in 2013 of more than $5,000,000,000, shares responsibility for enforcing the nation's civil immigration laws. ICE was formed in 2002 as part of the Homeland Security Act that resulted from the terrorist attacks of September 11, 2001. The number of deportations and removals of illegal immigrants within the interior of the country has grown over the last decade. In 2013, ICE processed 133,551 removals of individuals apprehended in the interior of the United States, in addition to the more than 200,000 it removed who were apprehended at the border.

Despite an increase in spending, border agents, fencing, and deportations, the number of unauthorized immigrants in the United States has grown fairly steadily in recent decades. As the authors of the viewpoints in this chapter illustrate, there is wide disagreement about the effectiveness of US immigration policies.

> "Washington has a responsibility to help resolve the conditions that the federal government helped create, with porous borders, burgeoning transnational crime, and millions living in the shadows."

The US-Mexican Border Needs Increased Security

The Heritage Foundation Immigration and Border Security Reform Task Force

In the following viewpoint, the Heritage Foundation Immigration and Border Security Reform Task Force argues that the border between the United States and Mexico needs to be improved by constructing the right infrastructure, supporting local law enforcement's efforts to police the border, utilizing the National Guard and the Coast Guard, adding the right technology, and cooperating with Mexico. The Immigration and Border Security Reform Task Force at the Heritage Foundation proposes policy reforms for immigration and border security.

"Advancing the Immigration Nation: Heritage's Positive Path to Immigration and Border Security Reform: The Heritage Foundation Immigration and Border Security Reform Task Force," *Backgrounder*, no. 2813, June 17, 2013, pp. 1–5. Copyright © 2013 The Heritage Foundation. All rights reserved. Reprinted with permission.

As you read, consider the following questions:

1. How many miles of fencing did the Secure Fence Act of 2006 authorize, according to the author?

2. What does the author claim is one of the best tools to facilitate cooperation between federal, state, local, and tribal authorities?

3. The Merida Initiative was established by President George W. Bush in 2008 to do what, according to the author?

Fixing America's broken southern border and deeply flawed immigration system is often framed as a stark choice between doing nothing or accepting a massive, sweeping, complicated bill that works at cross-purposes to its stated goals. Those are tragic options for the future of freedom, fiscal responsibility, and responsible governance. Americans should demand better.

An Alternative to Acquiescence

Today, Washington defaults to turning every big issue into Obamacare [referring to the Patient Protection and Affordable Care Act]—solutions that are labeled politically "too big to fail," but in practice not only fail to address root problems, but make those problems worse. Repeating this practice will be a disaster for immigration and border security. Worse, if Americans acquiesce to a "comprehensive" immigration bill, they will send Washington yet another signal that they are satisfied with a government that just does "something" rather than demanding governance that actually solves problems.

There are practical, effective, fair, and compassionate alternatives. Washington has simply never tried them. For many years, the Heritage Foundation has laid out a problem-solving road map for addressing the obstacles to immigration and border security reform. The principles behind these proposals have always been about fostering the freedom, security, and prosperity of all Americans in equal measure. In addition, the foundation's approach recognizes that Washington has a responsibility to help resolve the conditions that the federal government helped create, with porous borders, burgeoning transnational crime, and millions living in the shadows.

Immigration reform can move forward, focusing on commonsense initiatives that begin to address the practical challenges of immigration and border security. The key is to begin by working on the solutions on which everyone can agree rather than insisting on a comprehensive approach that divides Americans. Also, Washington must implement the mandates already on the books, follow through on existing initiatives, and employ the authorities that Congress has already granted before taking on new obligations. What is needed next is a piece-by-piece legislative agenda, implemented step-by-step that allows transparency, careful deliberation, and thoughtful implementation within responsible federal budgets.

A More Secure Border

A secure border between the U.S. and Mexico would be an engine for economic growth, facilitating the legitimate exchange of people, goods, and services. Moreover, it would serve as an obstacle to transnational crime and human trafficking, and facilitate the accurate and rapid targeting of national security threats. All of the measures that could help to build this kind of border can be achieved under existing law, faithfully fulfilling existing mandates for border security, and the regular order of congressional appropriations. Heritage has been advocating them for years. As a result of post-9/11 [referring to the September 11, 2001, terrorist attacks on the United States] initiatives, in 2007 Heritage concluded that "there already exist on the books numerous laws that, if enforced in a targeted manner, would discourage illegal immigration and the employment of undocumented labor, as well as send the signal that such activities will no longer be over-looked." They do not require complicated feel-good but meaningless metrics, massive new deficit spending, or bargaining amnesty for border security.

Constructing the Right Infrastructure. The Secure Fence Act of 2006 gave the federal government the authority to establish 700 miles of fencing on the U.S.-Mexico border. This mandate was never fully, adequately, or faithfully implemented. This is a serious shortfall. The key to employing the right combination of border obstacles, such as fencing, is careful assessment of operational needs and cost-benefit analysis. Effective border obstacles are expensive to construct and must be constantly monitored and patrolled.

Fencing is especially critical in areas with a low "melting point"—the time it takes for an individual to cross the border and "melt" into a landscape unnoticed. In urban border communities, spending money on physical barriers makes sense because individuals can easily cross the border and sneak quickly into the urban landscape, hiding in a building or stealing a car and driving away. Areas along high-trafficked smuggling routes are also good candidates. These areas are where border crossers are made to slow down, in order to allow the Border Patrol more time to identify and interdict them, and they are of the greatest benefit. Requirements for additional infrastructure should be driven by operational requirements and can be constructed under existing law and funded through the regular appropriations process.

In addition, a meaningful border security strategy would address investing in the infrastructure that facilitates legitimate trade and travel. Hundreds of millions of people cross U.S. borders each year in numbers approaching twice the population of the United States. The overwhelming majority travel through legal points of entry and exit, such as land border crossing points, airports, and harbors. Billions of tons of goods, accounting for a third of the U.S. gross domestic product (GDP), transit America's borders as well. Points of entry and exit must have the physical assets to support screening, inspection, and gathering, evaluating, and sharing of critical information.

Furthermore, adequate infrastructure—including bridges and roads, especially road networks that connect to rail terminals, seaports, and airports—is essential to providing the capacity, redundancy, and flexibility required to ensure that the free flow of trade and travel is not disrupted. This is particularly vital at the small number of transit nodes that handle most of the cross-border traffic.

Tackling the commercial infrastructure challenge does not require comprehensive immigration reform legislation either. Establishing priorities and providing revenue for these investments is not solely or, in many cases, even primarily a federal responsibility. For example, local governments own most of the 26 motor vehicle crossings on the Texas-Mexico border. Likewise, airports and seaports are owned and operated by a mix of public and private entities. An investment strategy will require more cooperative public-private partnerships, including targeting national transportation trust funds so that they are spent on national priorities rather than pork-barrel projects. Additionally, rather than relying heavily on subsidized public funding of infrastructure, investments should focus on "project-based" financing that shifts the risks and rewards to the private sector.

The Use of Local Law Enforcement

Supporting Local Law Enforcement. Many local law enforcement authorities on the border, particularly in rural communities, are on the front line of border security. In 2007, responding to reports of a disturbance in Arizona's Pima County, which shares a border with Mexico, officers encountered a grisly scene—two shot dead in a Dodge pickup truck, a woman in the front seat, a man sprawled in the back seat. A while later, officers found a third body, shot in the head and dragged into the desert. The killings, carried out by drug traffickers, were a wake-up call for the Pima County sheriff's office: Its turf had become the path of least resistance for those trafficking in drugs and people.

Border law enforcement agencies should receive robust federal grants to help address these challenges. Washington has poured billions into homeland security grants, yet it is not at all clear that this spending spree has done much to improve national preparedness or security. Unlike most homeland security grants (which have become exactly what the 9/11 Commission [formally known as the National Commission on Terrorist Attacks Upon the United States] warned against: "pork barrel" funding) or wasteful and ineffective programs, such as the Community Oriented Policing Services (COPS), taxpayers get far more bang for their homeland security bucks if more of the money is channeled where it is really needed—such as cooperative law enforcement initiatives to protect communities along the southern border. The Department of Homeland Security (DHS) already has a grant program to address this challenge—Operation Stonegarden. It just needs to be robustly funded and aggressively administered.

Taking a Teamwork Approach. Much of the criminal activity that crosses the border involves the use of networks that smuggle people, weapons, drugs, and money—making it a national security concern. Attacking these networks is key to reducing illicit cross-border trafficking. This requires the integrated cooperation of federal, state, local, and tribal authorities. One of the best tools to facilitate that cooperation is the Border Enforcement Security Task Force (BEST). BEST is a program that couples U.S. federal, state, and local law enforcement with Mexican law enforcement in order to share information and collaborate on matters such as border crime. Just this past December, President Barack Obama signed into law the Jaime Zapata Border Enforcement Security Task Force

Act, named after the Immigration and Customs Enforcement agent and BEST veteran who was killed in Mexico in 2011. DHS has yet to fully exercise its authorities under this law.

The Use of Other Partners

Encouraging Volunteers. Much like state and local governments, private citizens living in border communities recognized the need to take action at the border—border crimes and illegal immigration were having a direct impact on their neighborhoods and daily lives. Border ranchers, for instance, had had enough of illegal aliens destroying and stealing fencing and scaring cattle from watering holes. It is reasonable for private citizens to assist in vital government functions. Citizens can protect their property from crime, deter drug sales, and police border communities.

Legitimate concerns over liability, safety, and civil liberties can be addressed by encouraging a certain level of organization and accountability, which can be achieved through accreditation, official standards, and practical employment concepts consistent with volunteer service. The best way would be to encourage states to organize state defense forces (SDFs), volunteer organizations dedicated to assisting the government in a number of activities, including border control. These forces report to and are funded by state governments, are governed by state law, and report to the governor. California, New Mexico, and Texas already have SDFs. Legislation has been proposed in Arizona to create an SDF.

Support of the Guard. In 2006, President George W. Bush sent 6,000 National Guard troops to the southern border through a program called Operation Jump Start. These troops were deployed under Title 32 ("National Guard") of the United States Code, which means they served under the operational control of the governors, and were tasked with helping Border Patrol agents. When she served as governor of Arizona, Secretary of Homeland Security Janet Napolitano effectively used these forces to support security on the border. As U.S. Customs and Border Protection (CBP) became more successful in its recruiting efforts and its overall numbers rose, these troops were phased out. Under existing law, however, the administration can deploy these forces whenever they are needed to supplement manpower or other capabilities needed to reinforce border security efforts. National Guard forces can aid in border security activities through support during annual training periods. These deployments benefit guard units by providing additional training opportunities and can provide support to Border Patrol agents. Activities can be programmed in advance so they facilitate rather than disrupt other training and deployment requirements. During these operations, National Guard forces can remain under Title 32 status, which places control of these troops under the command of the state governor.

Adding the Right Technology. While DHS has had a troubled and controversial history adapting technology to the border, such as the deeply flawed implementation of the Secure Border Initiative Network (SBInet), the practices of the past 10 years are more than adequate as an assessment to determine which additional technologies would be the most efficacious. These include small unmanned aerial vehicles (UAVs) carrying a variety of sensors, which can be flown in U.S. airspace without compromising safety or privacy. In the end, SBInet did demonstrate the value of fixed sensors on towers when properly networked with the CBP for interdiction on high-traffic smuggling corridors. Elsewhere, mobile ground sensors and field-deployable biometrics, similar to systems used in Afghanistan, have proven effective for interdiction in remote areas. When DHS canceled SBInet in 2011, the department promised to develop a replacement system. This promise has not yet been met. DHS can acquire and employ the technologies to do so under existing budgets through regular appropriations. The department does not require additional congressional authorities to employ them.

Beyond the Land Border

Funding for the Coast Guard. An effective border strategy cannot focus exclusively on land borders. As land borders become more secure, drug smugglers and human traffickers will quickly look to sea options. Indeed, there is much evidence that this is already happening. Today, America is being invaded by "pangas"—small, open, outboard-powered boats that are a common fixture throughout Latin American ports. A typical small craft comes packed with a load of 1,500 pounds to 4,000 pounds of marijuana and a platoon of illegal immigrants. Many of those looking to enter the United States unlawfully are not looking for regular work. Often, they are gang members and other offenders with active warrants or criminal records who would not think of trying to slip through a land border crossing unnoticed. Small boat smuggling is a big problem in part because it is easy to hide the wolves among the sheep. There are more than 500,000 small recreational craft registered in the Southern California area alone.

Maritime efforts must be enhanced in conjunction with land security. The Coast Guard acts as the law enforcement for the high seas; however, it lacks the resources and capacities to do its job as effectively as it could. The Comprehensive Immigration Reform Bill does not address this challenge. The Coast Guard is funded through regular appropriations. Congress can support the Coast Guard by sufficiently funding the cutters, aircraft, equipment, and training that it needs to continue to protect America's seas and waterways.

Cooperating with Mexico. Addressing the challenges of safety, security, and sovereignty from both sides of the southern border is the most effective and efficient way to operationally control it. In 2008, President Bush established the Merida Initiative to facilitate cross-border cooperation on mutual interests of public safety and transnational crime. President Obama, however, has thoroughly failed to follow through and build on this initiative. This stands in sharp contrast to U.S.-Canadian cooperation on the northern border. Mexico is not an unwilling partner: The Mexican government has additional projects on the drawing board that include a new gendarme force that would be able to police rural areas and, potentially, a border patrol. Mexico also stems the flow of Central Americans across its southern border, many of whom have the U.S. as their intended destination.

There are a range of initiatives that could form the basis of a "Merida II," bringing the U.S. and Mexico closer together. The Obama administration could develop a broad master plan for U.S.-Mexican relations that coordinates law enforcement, judicial, and military assets to target transnational criminal organizations, gangs, human traffickers, terrorists, and other 21st-century threats to shared security. So, too, the administration could explore with Mexico specific agreements, protocols, and efforts that draw the two governments closer together in order to regularize and expedite legal movements of people and goods while increasing cross-border disincentives and obstacles to illegal activities, especially illegal migration. These initiatives could be implemented by executive action and do not require comprehensive immigration reform legislation.

> "Unchecked immigration and wide-
> spread noncompliance with the law is
> the by-product of our own failure to
> replace an outdated system."

No, We Don't Need More Immigration Enforcement

Gabriel Arana

In the following viewpoint, Gabriel Arana argues that it is not possible to completely secure the US borders and that calls for greater enforcement are misguided. Arana claims that the border has been adequately secured in recent years and more spending will not improve security. Arana contends that the immigration problem has little to do with border enforcement and more to do with an insufficient number of legal pathways for immigrants to come and work legally. Arana is a senior editor at the American Prospect.

As you read, consider the following questions:

1. The author cites a report showing that the United States spends how much annually on immigration enforcement?

2. Arana claims that immigration has been reduced to net zero after hitting a peak in what year?

3. According to the author, how many green cards does the United States allow each year for low-skilled workers?

If you need proof that nothing short of a Soviet-style blockade along our southern border will satisfy immigration hard-liners, look no further than Mark Krikorian, executive director of the Center for Immigration Studies—a think tank that, as the Southern Poverty Law Center points out, "has never found any aspect of immigration it liked." Krikorian has previously used his space at the *National Review Online* to grouse about the "unnatural" pronunciation of Sonia Sotomayor's name and to suggest that the United States slough off Puerto Rico to end the "gravy train." Last week [in January 2013], he used it to denounce a recent Migration Policy Institute report showing the United States spends approximately $18 billion per year on immigration enforcement, which exceeds federal spending on all other federal criminal law enforcement efforts combined.

Being the scrupulous researcher that he is, Krikorian hopped over to the websites of Immigration and Customs Enforcement (ICE) and Customs and Border Protection (CBP)—the two federal agencies whose primary responsibility is immigration enforcement—and found some press releases about cybercrime and drug smuggling. This naturally showed the report was lying because ICE and CBP don't spend *all* their money regulating immigration; they also enforce customs laws. Its authors, Krikorian concludes, were just cooking up numbers to support President [Barack] Obama's open-borders, amnesty agenda. His organization followed up with a press release saying much the same thing a few days later.

This convoluted logic and paranoia is typical of the research Krikorian's group puts out, but it illustrates an important point about the immigration debate: No amount of money or resources will ever be enough to convince the enforcement-first crowd that the border is finally "secure." This sets up a roadblock: So long as securing our borders is a precondition for tackling immigration reform, opponents can always claim—citing a recent crime committed by an immigrant or anecdotal evidence of border violence—that we're just not there yet. In effect, "enforcement first" ends up being "enforcement only."

In truth, it's impossible for an open society to totally seal its borders; in the regular course of conducting trade and allowing visitors and immigrants in and out, there will inevitably be people who end up in the country illegally and illicit contraband that slips in as well. But in the same way that we don't measure the success of our police forces by whether their jurisdictions are totally crime free, we shouldn't measure the efficacy of our immigration enforcement efforts by whether anyone is ever able to break our immigration laws.

By any reasonable standard, the unchecked immigration flow that began in the mid-1990s is now under control. We've doubled the number of Border Patrol agents in the last seven years and—to the chagrin of many immigrant rights advocates—deported undocumented immigrants at record rates. Apprehensions along the U.S.-Mexico border are at historic lows. Despite the fact that current quotas don't meet the current economic demand for immigrant labor, immigration enforcement and the sour U.S. job market have reduced immigration to *net zero* for the first time in 40 years, down from a peak of 525,000 in 2000. The increase in spending on immigration enforcement is even more dramatic if one goes back to 1986, when the Immigration Reform and Control Act ushered in the current era of immigration policy; since then, our spending on immigration has increased fifteenfold.

One can see the difference in resources allocated to border security since the 2007 push for immigration reform during George W. Bush's second term and especially since the 9/11

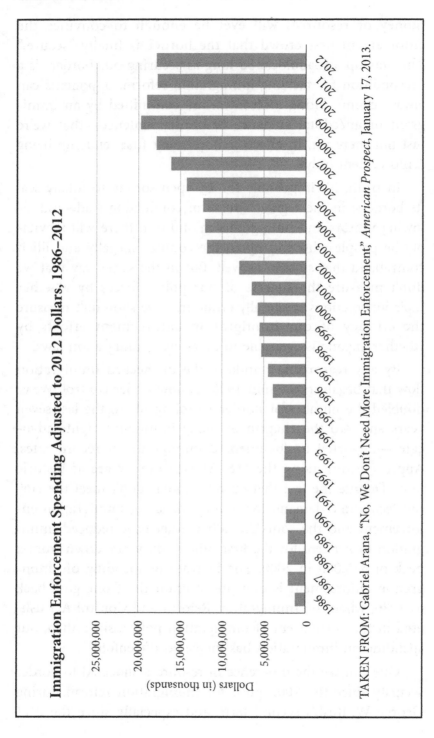

Immigration Enforcement Spending Adjusted to 2012 Dollars, 1986–2012

TAKEN FROM: Gabriel Arana, "No, We Don't Need More Immigration Enforcement," *American Prospect*, January 17, 2013.

attacks [referring to the September 11, 2001, terrorist attacks on the United States], after which funding for enforcement exploded. But the change in policy seems not to have registered with lawmakers, who are still talking about the ever-growing need for enforcement as if it were 2000. The fact is that we've dedicated ample resources to enforcement; the question is now how best to use them and what to do with the rest of the broken system.

Thankfully, it appears that Republicans in Congress, chastened by November's Latino wake-up call, may finally be abandoning the "enforcement-first" strategy. On Saturday, Senator Marco Rubio of Florida told the *Wall Street Journal* that he supports a "comprehensive solution" that would include increased enforcement as well as a path to citizenship for most of the 11 million immigrants estimated to be in the country illegally. Other Republican leaders, including Tea Party hero Paul Ryan, voiced their support for Rubio's plan.

For political reasons, Rubio is still calling for stricter enforcement, which gives immigration hawks cover to vote for a comprehensive bill. But the irony is that reforming the immigration system would significantly *reduce* the need for enforcement. Unchecked immigration and widespread noncompliance with the law is the by-product of our own failure to replace an outdated system. By ignoring labor demands—the United States only allots 5,000 green cards per year for low-skilled workers—and making legal immigration for certain classes of people (primarily low-skilled workers from Latin America) inordinately difficult, the current scheme encourages lawbreaking; rather than navigate the byzantine immigration process or wait 6 to 17 years to be reunited with family members, many immigrants choose to bypass the system altogether. Our failure to reform the immigration system has thus led to huge backlogs in the immigration courts and required the expansion of detention centers, which house approximately 33,000 people per day. Quite simply, making it easier to comply with the law would make more people do so, alleviating the burden on law enforcement and allowing them to concentrate on higher-priority removals. Think of a leaky bathtub: Instead of buying a new one, we're spending ever more money patching up the cracks. Replacing the thing means the repairman will have less work.

| *"Enforcement in the interior has fallen off alarmingly in the last several years."*

Immigration Enforcement in Sharp Decline, Despite Obama Administration's Claims

Jessica M. Vaughan

In the following viewpoint, Jessica M. Vaughan argues that in recent years the enforcement of immigration laws has declined, with fewer arrests of illegal immigrants and fewer deportations. Vaughan claims that this is not because there are fewer illegal immigrants in the country and contends that there is a need to boost enforcement of existing laws that allow the removal of illegal immigrants from the United States. Vaughan is director of policy studies for the Center for Immigration Studies.

As you read, consider the following questions:

1. According to the viewpoint, how many illegal border crossers were arrested in 2013?

2. According to Vaughan, how many illegal immigrants did Immigration and Customs Enforcement encounter in 2013 that *could* have been removed?

3. Vaughan claims that too many groups of illegal immigrants are considered off-limits for enforcement, citing what examples?

A fter nearly a year of a debate, Congress is at a stalemate over immigration reform. The Senate passed a bill that is unacceptable to the House, with too lenient an amnesty, too much new immigration, and too little enforcement, making it too costly for American workers. The Republican majority in the House wants to tackle the issue piece by piece, arguing that the first order of business should be shoring up enforcement and border security.

According to closely held metrics kept by the two main enforcement agencies in the Department of Homeland Security [DHS], House Republicans have a legitimate point. Border Patrol chief Michael Fisher recently disclosed at a conference that his agents arrested 420,000 illegal border crossers in 2013, marking the second straight year of increases and suggesting that significantly more people are trying to enter illegally over the southwest border, especially in South Texas. This admission upset [President Barack] Obama's political appointees at DHS, who had not yet decided how to explain this glaring contradiction of their claims that illegal immigration is a thing of the past.

Meanwhile, enforcement in the interior has fallen off alarmingly in the last several years. Leaked internal statistics show that Immigration and Customs Enforcement [ICE] agents are arresting many fewer illegal aliens inside the country, and removals from the interior have declined more than 35 percent since 2009. Arrests declined in every part of the country, with the biggest drops in Georgia and the Carolinas, where 62 percent fewer illegal aliens were picked up.

It's not because there are fewer illegal aliens to arrest. Experts agree that the size of the illegal population has not budged much in several years from about 11.5 million, and seems to be growing. It includes nearly 900,000 people like the president's uncle, who have been ordered removed at least once, but who refuse to leave because no one makes them.

These numbers call into question the Obama administration's claims of "record" deportations and "smarter" enforcement that they say surpass all previous administrations. These claims have been a key talking point for proponents of amnesty and the Senate bill, which sought to undercut enforcement in numerous ways. Advocates for illegal aliens, including the newly legalized "Dreamers," have taken to the streets and to the halls of the Capitol, staging vigils, confrontations and even disrupting the lighting of the Capitol Christmas tree, demanding a stop to all deportations.

As it turns out, the administration's claims of record deportations are "a little deceptive," as the president once told a group of Latino journalists. A little! Internal documents made public as part of a lawsuit by ICE officers against their own agency confirm that ICE has been padding its deportation numbers by taking credit for removing tens of thousands of illegal border crossers who were arrested by Border Patrol. They were held in ICE detention centers for just a few hours before removal. These cases represented about half of all deportations in the "record" counts of the last two years.

This is how the administration has been able to cover up plummeting interior arrests and give the false impression that they are vigorously enforcing immigration laws. In 2013, ICE agents encountered more than 700,000 aliens who could have been removed (which is a record, thanks to new resources from Congress). Most were found in jails. But they took action against fewer than 200,000; meaning that ICE is now releasing more illegal aliens—including criminal aliens—than it is arresting.

Exercising Prosecutorial Discretion

By this memorandum, I am setting forth how, in the exercise of our prosecutorial discretion, the Department of Homeland Security (DHS) should enforce the nation's immigration laws against certain young people who were brought to this country as children and know only this country as home. . . .

The following criteria should be satisfied before an individual is considered for an exercise of prosecutorial discretion pursuant to this memorandum:

- came to the United States under the age of sixteen;
- has continuously resided in the United States for a least five years preceding the date of this memorandum and is present in the United States on the date of this memorandum;
- is currently in school, has graduated from high school, has obtained a general education development certificate, or is an honorably discharged veteran of the Coast Guard or Armed Forces of the United States;
- has not been convicted of a felony offense, a significant misdemeanor offense, multiple misdemeanor offenses, or otherwise poses a threat to national security or public safety; and
- is not above the age of thirty.

Janet Napolitano,
"Exercising Prosecutorial Discretion with Respect to
Individuals Who Came to the United States as Children,"
US Department of Homeland Security, June 15, 2012.

This smoke-and-mirrors game is taking a toll on public safety and the rule of law. As ICE fills its scarce detention beds with illegal border crossers who could be more expeditiously dealt with by Border Patrol, political leaders in Washington order agents in the field to turn a blind eye to most illegal aliens living in our communities. Minor criminals, even chronic re-offenders, reckless or drunk drivers, those with families, those rejected for green cards, anyone claiming to have been brought as a child, and relatives of veterans are all considered off-limits for enforcement.

The official rationale for these policies, known as "prosecutorial discretion," is to keep ICE agents focused on removing dangerous criminal aliens rather than "harmless" illegal workers. But pols in ICE headquarters have created so many exceptions to the law that criminal removals have dropped too. In North Carolina alone, authorities have lost track of more than 3,000 illegal alien ex-cons that ICE failed to remove. Inevitably, they will find new victims.

The Obama administration's deliberate suppression of immigration enforcement has understandably chilled enthusiasm among House Republicans for a massive comprehensive bill that has to be passed to learn what's in it. Instead lawmakers should pass targeted measures to boost interior enforcement and restore credibility to the laws we have.

| "We must enforce our laws to protect and preserve the rights and freedoms that make America so great."

Trust but E-Verify

Lamar Smith

In the following viewpoint, Lamar Smith argues that failing to enforce immigration laws undermines the promise of freedom of the United States. Smith claims that the border must be secured, criminal immigrants must be deported, amnesty must not be granted to lawbreakers, and work-site immigration laws must be enforced. To prevent employers from hiring illegal immigrants, Smith endorses the Legal Workforce Act to require the use of E-Verify, a program that verifies legal work status of individuals. Smith is the US representative for Texas's twenty-first congressional district, serving since 1987.

As you read, consider the following questions:

1. According to Smith, what percentage of the US-Mexican border is under the operational control of the US Border Patrol?

2. Why does amnesty undermine the rule of law, according to the author?

3. According to Smith, how many US employers already voluntarily use E-Verify?

For centuries, immigrants have come to America seeking the promise of life, liberty, and the pursuit of happiness. Some came fleeing religious persecution. Others came for the possibility of a better life. But all were inspired by the freedoms that exist in the United States because of the rule of law.

Throughout our history, immigrants have contributed to American society and helped build the American dream. But today we face an immigration crisis. Lax enforcement of our immigration laws threatens the promise of life, liberty, and the pursuit of happiness that has made America what it is today. In order to protect the American dream, we must enforce our immigration laws.

According to a report by the Government Accountability Office, only 44 percent of the U.S.-Mexico border is under the "operational control" of the U.S. Border Patrol. Forty-four percent is a failing grade. Holes in the security of our borders threaten American lives. In Mexico, more than 35,000 people have been killed in the past five years. Without strong border security, this violence threatens to spill over into border towns, from Brownsville to San Diego. The first promise of the American dream is "life." In order to protect that promise, we must secure the U.S.-Mexico border.

We must also do more to protect Americans from criminal illegal immigrants. Although the [Barack] Obama administration has increased the deportation of criminal immigrants, two Supreme Court rulings created a safe haven for dangerous criminal immigrants who cannot be removed. Because these rulings prohibit criminal immigrants from being detained longer than six months if they cannot be deported, federal officials have been forced to release thousands of criminal im-

The Proposed Legal Workforce Act

Not later than the date that is 6 months after the date of the enactment of the Legal Workforce Act, an employer shall make an inquiry, as provided in subsection (d), using the verification system to seek verification of the identity and employment eligibility of any individual described in clause (ii) employed by the employer whose employment eligibility has not been verified under the E-Verify program described in section 403(a) of the Illegal Immigration Reform and Immigrant Responsibility Act of 1996.

H.R. 1772, 113th Congress,
1st Session, April 26, 2013.

migrants into our communities. Tragically, many have gone on to commit more crimes, including murder. That's why I introduced the Keep Our Communities Safe Act to prevent the release of dangerous criminal immigrants back into our neighborhoods.

The promise of "liberty" for those who come to America is also threatened by illegal immigration. People from around the world come to the U.S. seeking freedom from oppression. These individuals come the right way—they follow our laws and wait in line for America's freedoms and opportunities. Citizenship is the highest honor our nation can bestow. We should not cheapen it by giving it away to individuals who broke our laws to come here in the first place.

But that's precisely what amnesty does: It undermines the rule of law. We have succeeded as a nation in preserving our liberties because we adhere to the rule of law. We punish law-breakers in order to protect the freedoms of law-abiders. Amnesty does the exact opposite—it rewards criminal behavior and encourages more illegal immigration.

For many, the pursuit of happiness is also the pursuit of prosperity. Part of the American dream is the ability to provide for your family, have a job that pays the bills, and puts a roof over your head. The last few years of economic uncertainty have made this dream harder to attain for millions of U.S. citizens and legal immigrants. Twenty-four million Americans are unemployed or underemployed. Meanwhile, there are 7 million illegal workers with jobs in the U.S. We could open up millions of jobs for citizens and legal immigrants if we simply enforced work-site immigration laws.

E-Verify is a program that helps preserve scarce jobs for U.S. citizens and legal immigrants. It allows employers to check whether prospective employees are legally authorized to work in the U.S. The program is free, quick, and easy to use—persons eligible to work are immediately confirmed 99.5 percent of the time. More than 270,000 employers across the U.S. voluntarily use E-Verify, and an average of 1,300 new businesses sign up each week. I've introduced the Legal Workforce Act to require all U.S. employers to use E-Verify. This bill is one of the most significant steps we can take to preserve the pursuit of happiness for millions of U.S. citizens and legal immigrants while curbing incentives for future illegal immigrants.

The U.S. has been and will continue to be a nation of immigrants. But we are also a nation of laws. And we must enforce our laws to protect and preserve the rights and freedoms that make America so great.

Periodical and Internet Sources Bibliography

The following articles have been selected to supplement the diverse views presented in this chapter.

Michael Bargo Jr.	"Federal Enforcement, Not Immigration Reform, Is Needed," *American Thinker*, May 4, 2013.
Aura Bogado	"Five Things to Know About Immigration and Enforcement," *Nation*, February 20, 2013.
Emily Chertoff	"Deport the Interlopers? But They've Been Here All Along," *Atlantic*, January 30, 2013.
Federation for American Immigration Reform (FAIR)	"US Mexico Border Fence and Patrol Operations," 2013.
John Allen Gay	"E-Verify, G-Verify, and Immigration Reform," *National Interest*, June 28, 2013.
Peter Kirsanow	"Illegal Immigration, Irresponsibility, and Terrorism," *National Review Online*, June 25, 2013.
Mark Krikorian	"Border Fencing: One Tool Among Many," *National Review Online*, March 28, 2014.
Natasha Lennard	"US Spends Vast Amounts Enforcing Immigration," *Salon*, January 8, 2013.
Alex Newman	"Feds Purposely Keeping U.S. Borders Wide Open, Experts Say," *New American*, February 20, 2012.
Cathy Reisenwitz	"E-Verify Turns Work into a Privilege, and Empowers the Surveillance State," Reason.com, November 17, 2013.
Michael Todd	"America's Imaginary Border Insecurity," *Salon*, May 11, 2013.

CHAPTER 3

Are Illegal Immigrants Treated Justly?

Chapter Preface

One controversial issue in the illegal immigration debate involves the children of unauthorized immigrants. Under the Fourteenth Amendment to the US Constitution, children born in the United States to illegal immigrants, as all others born in the United States, are granted US citizenship: "All persons born or naturalized in the United States, and subject to the jurisdiction thereof, are citizens of the United States and of the State wherein they reside." However, many unauthorized immigrant children are brought to the United States by their parents. Unlike their parents, they cannot rightfully be said to have broken the law on their own accord. This has caused some to propose different policies for these unauthorized immigrant children.

A US Supreme Court ruling several decades ago determined that public education may not be denied to the children of illegal immigrants. The decision was not universally supported and continues to be condemned by many. The 1982 case of *Plyler v. Doe* involved a Texas law that withheld state funds from educating illegal immigrant children, permitting school districts to deny these children enrollment. For almost a century, it has been state policy that all children residing in the United States legally have a right to a public education. The court in *Plyler* argued that there was no good justification for a state to withhold this right from children brought to the country illegally by their parents, determining that the equal protection clause of the Fourteenth Amendment protects illegal immigrant children from unequal treatment.

Since the decision in *Plyler*, all states have been required to provide all children access to the public education system, regardless of legal status. According to the Pew Research Center, unauthorized immigrant children make up 2.5 percent of students in US elementary and secondary schools. Many worry that offering free public education to the children of illegal immigrants encourages people to break the law and is unfair to American taxpayers. Still others claim that it is unfair to deny an unauthorized immigrant child an education because of the actions of the child's parents.

There is a similar controversy regarding proposals to address the legal status of these children when they come of age. The Development, Relief, and Education for Alien Minors Act (DREAM Act), proposed numerous times in Congress since 2001 but not passed, would allow illegal immigrant children access to permanent residency. Different versions of the bill have included different educational, moral, and time-limit requirements. On June 15, 2012, after the failure by Congress to pass the DREAM Act, the Barack Obama administration issued a memorandum implementing the policy of Deferred Action for Childhood Arrivals (DACA). DACA does not offer legal status, but it directs US Customs and Border Protection (CBP), US Citizenship and Immigration Services (USCIS), and US Immigration and Customs Enforcement (ICE) to defer removal proceedings against certain unauthorized immigrants who were brought to the United States as children.

As the authors of the viewpoints in this chapter illustrate, controversy abounds on the issue of justice for unauthorized immigrants. Both for the adults who came to the United States on their own accord and for the children they brought with them in some cases, there is little consensus on whether or not the United States is treating these individuals justly.

| *"This is an issue of fairness, decency, and compassion."*

It Is Unfair to Deny Innocent Immigrant Children Legal Status

Cory Gardner

In the following viewpoint, Cory Gardner argues that new legislation is needed to fix the nation's broken immigration system. Gardner contends that an important part of reform is to grant legal status to children brought illegally to the United States. He claims that this should be part of a reform package that includes securing the border and using E-Verify, while not rewarding adults who break the law by entering the United States illegally. Gardner has served as the Republican US representative for Colorado's fourth congressional district since 2011.

As you read, consider the following questions:

1. What piece of legislation does Gardner charge with helping to result in approximately eleven million people in the United States without documentation?

Cory Gardner, Testimony, "Addressing the Immigration Status of Illegal Immigrants Brought to the United States as Children," Subcommittee on Immigration and Border Security, Committee on the Judiciary, US House of Representatives, July 23, 2013.

2. What two things does the author say must occur prior to granting legal status to children brought to the United States illegally?

3. What reason does the author give for opposing in-state tuition for illegal immigrants?

The Immigration Reform and Control Act of 1986 proved unworkable and too easily avoidable, and it helped result in approximately eleven million people in the United States without documentation. We need long-term, commonsense legislation to fix this broken system. The House [of Representatives] is committed to moving forward with a step-by-step process, with proper deliberation and debate surrounding each piece of reform. It is important that we do this right— proving to the American people the federal government can be trusted to build a lasting system that cannot simply be put aside because it is unworkable or the political will is simply not present to make it work.

The Current Immigration Laws

This afternoon [July 23, 2013], I will share my views on how to move forward. I believe any immigration reform effort must begin first with border security and enforcement of the law. A strong guest-worker program, accompanied by a modernized E-Verify system, is critical. I will also discuss the potential reform for the very young—children—who were brought illegally into this country as minors, and possible ways to address this issue.

Many of us elected in 2010 came to Congress because we wanted to put this nation back to work. We wanted to get government out of the way in order to grow the economy so that people can find jobs and make sure there is a better tomorrow. We came to Washington to keep the American dream alive and ensure that this great nation serves as a beacon of hope for individuals and families that want to achieve the American dream.

The DREAM Act

These are young people who study in our schools, they play in our neighborhoods, they're friends with our kids, they pledge allegiance to our flag. They are Americans in their hearts, in their minds, in every single way but one: on paper. They were brought to this country by their parents—sometimes even as infants—and often have no idea that they're undocumented until they apply for a job or a driver's license, or a college scholarship.

Put yourself in their shoes. Imagine you've done everything right your entire life—studied hard, worked hard, maybe even graduated at the top of your class—only to suddenly face the threat of deportation to a country that you know nothing about, with a language that you may not even speak.

That's what gave rise to the DREAM [Development, Relief, and Education for Alien Minors] Act. It says that if your parents brought you here as a child, if you've been here for five years, and you're willing to go to college or serve in our military, you can one day earn your citizenship. . . .

Now, both parties wrote this legislation. And a year and a half ago, Democrats passed the DREAM Act in the House, but Republicans walked away from it. It got 55 votes in the Senate, but Republicans blocked it. The bill hasn't really changed. The need hasn't changed. It's still the right thing to do.

"Remarks by the President on Immigration,"
The White House, Office of the Press Secretary, June 15, 2012.

It has been said many times before—the United States is a nation of immigrants. Had I not been blessed to have been born in this country, I know I would have done everything I could to make sure my family had the opportunity to grow up here. We are also a nation of laws. Our current immigration laws have proven inadequate and are not being enforced. If a law is not enforced or it is ignored, then we no longer remain a nation of laws and the law becomes worth little more than the paper upon which it is written. According to the *Wall Street Journal*, between forty and forty-two percent of the undocumented people in this country came here legally, but overstayed their visas. We need to move forward by building a new system of immigration laws that will stand strong and secure, but still allow a workable system for people that want to be a part of this great nation and healthy economy to have the opportunity to do so. I urge the House to be compassionate and fair during this process.

Border security and interior enforcement remain my top priority during this debate—it must come first. A government that cannot secure its own border is a government that is not doing its job. The same is with a government that cannot assure a legal workforce. In 1986, the American people were promised interior enforcement during immigration overhaul, but this never took place. Ignoring immigration laws for at least two decades has resulted in at least eleven million undocumented individuals throughout the nation. We can rebuild the trust of the American people by securing the borders and enforcing the laws, and making sure that no one can simply choose not to enforce the law or waive it through administrative process. Not only do strong security and enforcement measures need to exist in any reform, but there must be confirmation from a credible, outside entity that these measures have been satisfied and implemented.

A Proposal for Child Immigrants

Once we have secured our borders and are enforcing laws—knowing the measures are working—we may look to other reform provisions. Today, we are here to specifically discuss those amongst us who were brought to the country as young children. These individuals, for all intents and purposes, are culturally American. These are the young adults and children who grew up in the United States and go to school with our children and grandchildren, with my daughter. These children know no other nation, except for the United States.

This is an issue of fairness, decency, and compassion. Their parents made a decision to enter this country illegally and our broken system did not prevent it. They deserve to be afforded some form of legal status that recognizes that they are here through no fault of their own. It is not their fault, nor was it their decision to not follow the law. I believe members across the aisle can unite and agree that providing these children with some sort of immigration relief is the just and fair thing to do. But it must be part of a step-by-step reform package.

Any legislation that would address these children would need to be solely for the benefit of the child, and no one else. It cannot elicit chain migration. During this process, we must find the appropriate balance between compassion and justice. While these children remain innocent, we cannot reward those family members who have broken the law. However, the children do deserve to have the opportunity to continue the American dream and we, as members of Congress, should have the compassion to provide them with this.

The Overall Need for Immigration Reform

In 2005, I had just been appointed to the state legislature. I held one of my first town meetings on the eastern plains of Colorado in a small farm town. The government teacher of the local school brought the senior government class to attend the meeting. During the question-and-answer portion of the meeting, a young girl stood up and introduced herself, proudly stating that she was graduating first in her class, the valedictorian. She had gone to school with her classmates, in the same school, since kindergarten. But, she said, she was brought into this country when she was only a few months old and she was illegal. "Do you support in-state tuition for illegal aliens?" she asked.

I told her that I did not, because allowing passage of such a policy was avoiding the real problem, it was not addressing the overall need for immigration reform. We must pursue meaningful immigration reform to fix the broken nature of the process before anything like this can happen.

A month ago, on the eastern plains of Colorado, I saw this same girl. The valedictorian of her class, waiting tables. Eight years later, I once again talked about the need for immigration reform. Eight years later, nothing has happened.

This time, Congress cannot just talk about reform. We must do it.

While there will be strong disagreement about what to do, how to proceed, and what the end policy will ultimately look like, we cannot simply do nothing. We must act. And I believe we can do so in a way that, thirty years from now, future generations of this country—both immigrants and non-immigrants—can say, they did it right. It is working.

> "There is a fundamental principle that parents are responsible for the consequences that their actions and choices have on their kids."

It Is Immoral to Grant Illegal Immigrant Children Legal Status

Ira Mehlman

In the following viewpoint, Ira Mehlman argues that there are several moral arguments against passing legislation that grants the children of illegal immigrants any kind of legal status. Mehlman claims that the DREAM (Development, Relief, and Education for Alien Minors) Act rewards parents for illegal behavior and encourages more foreign parents to bring their children to the United States illegally. Mehlman claims that the situation is unfortunate for illegal immigrant children, but it is not the responsibility of the United States to fix. Mehlman is media director for the Federation for American Immigration Reform (FAIR).

As you read, consider the following questions:

1. According to Mehlman, what is the fundamental premise driving the moral argument *in favor* of the DREAM Act?

2. For what reason does Mehlman claim that the amnesty created by legislation such as the DREAM Act would have to be repeated?

3. The author claims that not giving illegal immigrant children legal residence does not amount to punishment for what reason?

It's back. Sen. Dick Durbin (D-Ill.) is once again pushing the DREAM [Development, Relief, and Education for Alien Minors] Act amnesty. Before a packed room (mostly of illegal aliens), the Senate Judiciary Committee held a hearing earlier this week [in June of 2011] stacked with witnesses who favor granting amnesty to millions of illegal aliens.

Leaving aside all of the deceitful provisions that have been built into the bill that makes it a much broader amnesty than proponents let on, it is important to address the fundamental premise that passing the bill is a moral imperative because the people who would benefit are blameless for being here illegally.

Five Moral Arguments Against the DREAM Act

The DREAM Act fulfills the parents' principle reason for breaking the law in the first place. Ask the typical illegal alien why he or she came to the United States illegally and invariably the answer is, "I wanted to do better for my family." This is a perfectly rational and understandable response, but not a justification for violating the law. In essence, what the DREAM Act does is provide the parents precisely what they sought when they brought their kids illegally to the United States: a green

© Terry Wise/Cartoonstock.com.

card and all of the benefits that America has to offer. Even if the bill were to include a provision that DREAM Act beneficiaries could never sponsor the parents who brought them to the country illegally, it would still fulfill the parents' primary objective for bringing them here.

The DREAM Act would touch off an even greater wave of illegal immigration. Because the DREAM Act is being marketed as a moral imperative—as opposed to a more general amnesty, which is sold as bowing to reality—it comes with an absolute assurance that it will be repeated. If we have a moral imperative to provide amnesty to the current population of people who were brought here as kids, won't we have the same moral imperative for the next generation of people who arrive under similar circumstances? The unmistakable message to people all around the world is: Get over here and bring your kids. America will feel morally obligated to give them green cards too.

The DREAM Act absolves illegal aliens of their fundamental responsibilities as parents. There is a fundamental principle that parents are responsible for the consequences that their actions and choices have on their kids. Unfortunately, children inevitably pay a price when parents make bad decisions or break laws. The DREAM Act carves out a single exception to this universal tenet of the social contract. The message it sends is that if you violate U.S. immigration law, American society is responsible for fixing the mess you created for your kids.

The absence of a reward or benefit is not the same as a punishment. DREAM Act proponents repeatedly argue that by not granting legal status to targeted beneficiaries we are, essentially, punishing children for the sins of their parents. This is an absolutely specious claim. By no stretch of the imagination are the children of illegal aliens being punished. Not rewarding them with legal residence and expensive college tuition subsidies is simply withholding benefits to which they never had any entitlement in the first place.

Adults have the obligation to do the right thing, even if their parents have done the wrong thing. Society glorifies people who do what is right, especially when doing what is right comes at some significant cost. Yes, many would-be DREAM Act beneficiaries have been dealt a bad hand (by their parents). As difficult (even unfair) as it may be, upon reaching adulthood they have the responsibility to obey the law. When, for example, Jose Antonio Vargas proclaims on the pages of the *New York Times Magazine* that he knowingly engaged in illegal activities in order to remain and work in the United States illegally, he became culpable in his own right. While he, and others like him, may be more sympathetic than the people who committed the predicate offense, their situation does not excuse their own illegal acts.

> *"The bill gives an opportunity for current undocumented immigrants who otherwise qualify for enlistment to give back to the nation that has provided them with so much."*

Immigrant Children Should Earn Legal Status Through Military Service

Jeff Denham

In the following viewpoint, Jeff Denham argues that legislation should be passed to allow adults brought to the United States illegally as children to join the US military in order to serve the country and gain permanent residence. Denham contends that the US military has always allowed foreign nationals to serve in the armed forces as a pathway to American citizenship, and young undocumented immigrants should be granted this privilege as well. Denham is the Republican US representative for California's tenth congressional district.

Jeff Denham, Testimony, "Addressing the Immigration Status of Illegal Immigrants Brought to the United States as Children," Subcommittee on Immigration and Border Security, Committee on the Judiciary, US House of Representatives, July 23, 2013.

As you read, consider the following questions:

1. What fraction of US Army enlistees in the 1840s were immigrants, according to the author?

2. What current legislation allows foreigners in the United States on student visas and employment-based visas to join the armed forces and earn citizenship?

3. What is the name of the legislation that Denham proposes?

As a resident of central California, I have spent several decades getting an education, running a business, raising children, farming, attending worship services, volunteering for school events and kids' sports events—all alongside neighbors who were immigrants from Central America, South America, Southeast Asia, Portugal, and many other parts of the world.

I have also witnessed the trials and joys of immigration through my own family. My father-in-law is a naturalized citizen from Mexico, and my wife and her siblings are first-generation Americans. Watching my father-in-law and other family members go through the process of becoming citizens and integrating their pride of their heritage seamlessly with their American patriotism has helped shape my idea of what patriotism means. I am grateful for the opportunities I have had to experience the rich heritage of immigrants in one of the most diverse regions of the world, and it is a heritage my wife and I have taken great care to share with our two children and our nieces and nephews.

Immigrants in the U.S. Military

Although I grew up in a very diverse environment, it was during my 16 years serving in the United States Air Force that I developed my strongest appreciation for the contribution of immigrants to our nation. I served alongside many foreign nationals who were able to earn citizenship through putting their lives on the line for Americans in the armed services.

Our nation has never made citizenship a requirement for service in our armed forces. Since the founding of our nation, noncitizens have been a part of our military, and Congress has seen fit to make military service a way for patriotic individuals from other countries to show allegiance to our flag and become United States citizens.

Almost half of U.S. Army enlistees in the 1840s were immigrants and more than 660,000 military veterans became citizens through naturalization between 1862 and 2000. These men and women have proven that they are prepared to make the ultimate sacrifice for their adopted country. I believe that anyone who swears an oath to defend our nation and serves out an enlistment term honorably should be entitled to the privileges afforded to American citizens.

Currently, citizens of the Marshall Islands, Micronesia and Palau, as well as American Samoa, can gain citizenship through military service. Many individuals here on student visas and employment-based visas have special eligibility to join our armed forces and earn citizenship through the Military Accessions Vital to the National Interest (MAVNI) program. Additionally, many foreign nationals and legal permanent residents serve in our armed forces as a way to earn citizenship. In the 1950s, Congress passed the now expired Lodge[-Philbin] Act, which allowed the military to recruit from Europe and other nations overseas. Between 1952 and 1990, 34,620 Filipinos enlisted in the navy and were granted U.S. citizenship. In all of these cases, national security is enhanced, not threatened or undermined by foreign nationals and noncitizens. Likewise, allowing undocumented immigrants to enlist would not pose any additional national security risk because they would be subject to the same screening mechanisms in place for the other foreign nationals serving in our armed forces to earn the right to be called Americans.

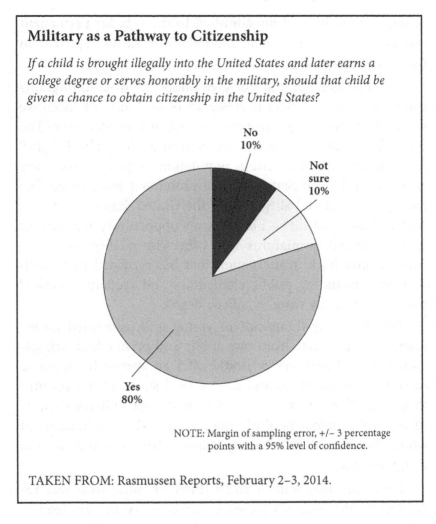

Military as a Pathway to Citizenship

If a child is brought illegally into the United States and later earns a college degree or serves honorably in the military, should that child be given a chance to obtain citizenship in the United States?

No
10%

Not
sure
10%

Yes
80%

NOTE: Margin of sampling error, +/– 3 percentage points with a 95% level of confidence.

TAKEN FROM: Rasmussen Reports, February 2–3, 2014.

The ENLIST Act

In order to allow undocumented [immigrants] to serve our country, I introduced [on June 14, 2013] the ENLIST [Encourage New Legalized Immigrants to Start Training] Act, H.R. 2377, which authorizes the enlistment in the armed forces of undocumented immigrants who were brought into the United States as children and who are otherwise qualified for enlistment. This bill will provide a way for the undocumented immigrants to be lawfully admitted to the U.S. for permanent residence by reason of their honorable service and sacrifice in the U.S. military.

The ENLIST Act will not give undocumented immigrants special benefits, nor will it create an opportunity or incentive for undocumented immigrants to rush the border now. The bill will not change military naturalization law. The ENLIST Act will only affect a certain population of people who have been in the United States and are prohibited from expressing their patriotism and allegiance to the United States under current military code. The bill gives an opportunity for current undocumented immigrants who otherwise qualify for enlistment to give back to the nation that has provided them with so much, including public elementary and secondary education and, in many cases, a college degree.

For the many thousands of young undocumented immigrants who graduate from our public and private high schools each year, military service would offer an avenue for them to serve the United States and earn a legal status in the country they love. These recruits would provide the military departments with a talent pool of young men and women, many of whom would have strategically valuable language and cultural competencies.

I recently met with a constituent of mine who was recruited by the marines to serve our country for her leadership, aptitude, skills, courage, and patriotism. Through the course of the recruitment process, she discovered for the first time that she does not have a Social Security number because she was brought unlawfully into the United States, even though her siblings were born here, are American citizens, and serve our country in the military. She would have been able to serve her country had my ENLIST Act already been law. It is a shame to see siblings of our service men and women denied the ability to put their lives on the line for our country. Congress has an interest in helping build up and care for our armed services, and that includes providing opportunities for patriotic young people like this young woman to enlist and serve alongside our forefathers and the greatest heroes of American history.

This body is debating different approaches to fixing our broken immigration system, but one thing we should all agree on is that the approach must require those who came here illegally to give back before they can receive any additional benefit. As someone who has served, I remember the pride I felt to wear the uniform and cannot think of any better way for these young people to earn the right to fully share in the rights and freedoms of America.

> "The ... administration is working dili-
> gently to make all violations of the im-
> migration law into secondary offenses."

Obama's Immigration Fiat

Mark Krikorian

*In the following viewpoint, Mark Krikorian argues that it is a
mistake to undermine immigration law by failing to deport most
illegal immigrants under the justification of prioritization. Krikorian claims that although some prioritization is necessary, the
Barack Obama administration has gone too far in failing to use
random enforcement to uphold the current immigration laws
and allowing too many exceptions. Krikorian is the executive director of the Center for Immigration Studies.*

As you read, consider the following questions:

1. What analogy does the author give to illustrate the
   problem with making all violations of immigration law
   into secondary offenses?

2. According to Krikorian, how many illegal immigrants
   already in the deportation pipeline will have their cases
   reexamined?

3. What fraction of illegal immigrants does the author claim snuck across the border?

Most U.S. states require all those riding in an automobile to wear seat belts. But failure to wear a seat belt is usually a "secondary offense," meaning that you cannot be pulled over and ticketed solely for that infraction but instead must be pulled over for speeding or some other offense first.

The Obama administration is working diligently to make all violations of the immigration law into secondary offenses. The goal is to ensure that no illegal immigrant, ever, is removed from the United States solely for being an illegal immigrant. Rather, only those illegal immigrants guilty of some additional crime—and a "serious" crime, at that—should be deported.

This is the equivalent of the Internal Revenue Service announcing that ordinary citizens who fail to pay their taxes would suffer no consequences because the IRS would pursue only those who commit *additional* crimes, such as drug dealing or terrorism.

Although the administration hasn't formally announced this secondary-offense approach as the overarching framework for immigration policy, its specific actions and announcements over the past two and a half years leave no room for doubt.

The first indication of this came at the beginning of President Obama's term, when further work-site raids by immigration agents were prohibited. In order to maintain the pretense of work-site enforcement, the administration increased audits of employers' personnel records, requiring those workers who were illegal to be fired. By design [1] however, this approach scrupulously avoids the arrest of any illegal workers, enabling them to just get another job down the street.

The Justice Department's lawsuits against Arizona and Alabama are part of the same pattern. Both states passed tough immigration laws that would have resulted in local police identifying ordinary illegal aliens and reporting them to federal authorities. But this ran contrary to the policy that all illegal immigrants must be permitted to remain here unmolested until they commit some additional, non-immigration-related offense—and so, the federal government joined the ACLU [American Civil Liberties Union] and other administration allies in suing to stop the legislation. The lower courts have ruled against Arizona, which has filed an appeal to the Supreme Court, while the Alabama law is temporarily on hold as the judge in the case examines the arguments in more detail. If any part of the Alabama law is upheld, the Supreme Court would be more likely to hear the Arizona case so as to ensure a single standard across the federal court system. But even if the Supreme Court hears the case and finds for Arizona, the immigration authorities can simply choose not to deport those reported to them by local police.

Then in June of this year, Immigration and Customs Enforcement (ICE) issued a memo [2] encouraging field agents to exercise "prosecutorial discretion" in considering which aliens to arrest—a thinly veiled order not to arrest illegal immigrants meeting any of various criteria. Most of the objection to this action stemmed from the fact that the first several criteria listed covered those who would have been eligible for the DREAM Act amnesty, which would have legalized certain illegal immigrants who came here before age sixteen; Congress rejected the DREAM Act and here, critics said, the administration was simply enacting it by fiat.

The critics were right; the administration had committed what can only be described as a lawless act. But obscured by the debate over the de facto implementation of the DREAM Act were the other criteria in the memo which effectively ensured that *all* illegal immigrants would be exempt from deportation until they had killed someone or committed some other violent crime. Those who should be exempted include illegal aliens who have "ties and contributions to the community, including family relationships," those with "a U.S. citizen or permanent resident spouse, child, or parent," illegal aliens who are minors, or elderly, or ill, or married to someone who's ill, or the primary caretaker for a minor, or pregnant, or nursing, or who has few ties to his home country, or whose home country is unstable, etc., etc.

The most recent manifestation of the policy was the August announcement that those illegal aliens who had been arrested before the above-mentioned prosecutorial discretion policy went into effect—i.e., were already in the deportation pipeline—should all have their cases reexamined, and those who aren't rapists or drug dealers should be released. This applies to 300,000 people, and while not all will benefit, those who do will actually be given the legal right to work and a Social Security number—an administrative amnesty [3], albeit without the immediate prospect of citizenship.

The result of all this is that the steady increase in deportations we'd seen since the Clinton administration has stalled and started to reverse; in FY 2007, there were about 319,000 "removals," 360,000 in FY08, 395,000 in FY09 (the first third of which was still in the Bush term), 387,000 last fiscal year and we're likely to see a further drop this year.

Rather than openly defending their secondary-offense approach to immigration, administration spokesmen have argued that they have limited resources and must prioritize among so many illegal aliens, and the most dangerous should be first in line for removal. The problem with this claim is that this administration is the first in a long time not to request additional deportation funding—in other words, it's pleading poverty, but a poverty of its own making.

Despite that, resources will never be unlimited and some prioritization will always be necessary. But there are still two problems with using prioritization as political cover for its secondary-offense approach. First, other law enforcement agencies prioritize all the time without pulling the plug on random enforcement; tax audits, for instance, do not focus exclusively on money launderers, drug dealers and corporate crooks but also on a random selection of ordinary taxpayers to ensure that people know there's a chance that they'll be caught if they cheat. The same is true for enforcement of traffic laws, occupational safety and health laws, hunting regulations and every other kind of enforcement—except immigration.

Secondly, the idea that even ordinary illegal aliens are "otherwise law-abiding" is simply false. To begin with, two-thirds of the illegal population snuck across the border, which is a crime; the other third overstayed their visas, which is merely a civil infraction, like a traffic ticket. But both visa-overstayers and border-jumpers commit identity fraud and identity theft, perjury (if they submitted false information for employment), tax fraud, false claims of U.S. citizenship, failure to register for the draft, various kinds of conspiracy and so on. In the end, almost every illegal alien has committed multiple felonies for which less favored categories of people, such as U.S. citizens or legal immigrants, would surely be prosecuted.

The administration's individual actions and announcements on immigration have occasioned plenty of angry comment. But whether this illegal alien gets amnesty or that illegal alien is released from detention is secondary to the larger problem—the downgrade of immigration law itself. And since immigration control is one of the most important security tools [4], not only is the rule of law compromised, but our nation's safety as well.

Links

1. http://www.nationalreview.com/corner/274669/half-measures-dont-work-mark-krikorian

2. http://www.ice.gov/doclib/secure-communities/pdf/prosecutorial-discretion-memo.pdf

3. http://www.nationalreview.com/articles/273352/obama-s-administrative-amnesty-lamar-smith

4. http://nationalinterest.org/article/keeping-terror-out-710

> *"Obama could instantly—and perma-*
> *nently—legalize millions of illegal im-*
> *migrants."*

Law-Abiding Illegal Immigrants Do Not Need to Be Deported

Keegan Hamilton

In the following viewpoint, Keegan Hamilton argues that the politics of immigration reform is keeping the Barack Obama administration from stopping all costly detention and deportation proceedings against noncriminal illegal immigrants. Hamilton contends that although somewhat controversial, the president can and has used prosecutorial discretion to release illegal immigrant detainees and to direct immigration agencies to defer deportation proceedings against certain classes of illegal immigrants, such as childhood arrivals. Hamilton is a journalist.

As you read, consider the following questions:

1. According to Hamilton, how many illegal immigrant detainees were set free due to $3.2 billion in sequester-mandated budget cuts?

2. How much does it cost the government for detention and deportation per illegal immigrant deported, according to Hamilton?

3. The author claims that if immigration reform were to fail, what could President Barack Obama do under prosecutorial discretion?

In February [2013], the Department of Homeland Security [DHS] began quietly releasing immigrants from federal detention centers across the country. There was no clear pattern to the releases: Several hundred people were allowed to walk free from facilities in Texas and Arizona, while no more than 50 were freed from the sprawling prison south of Seattle that houses nearly 1,300 undocumented people from around the globe.

For immigration advocates, it was a conspicuous but not wholly unusual departure from business as usual by the feds.

The Release of Detainees

"It's hard to pinpoint what the reasons were for the releases," says Jorge Barón, director of the Northwest Immigrant Rights Project, an organization that provides legal aid to undocumented people. "This is not a causative thing. It's fluid. People get released all the time."

The releases were not announced publicly, and DHS officials initially refused to confirm the move, which involved mostly low-risk individuals accused of overstaying their visas, traffic offenses, and other minor transgressions. Later, the agency insisted only a few hundred people were temporarily released on bond. When it finally emerged that 2,228 immigrants were set free, in part because of $3.2 billion in sequester-mandated budget cuts, the backlash was histrionic, even by Capitol Hill standards.

House Judiciary Committee chairman Bob Goodlatte called the releases "abhorrent" and accused President [Barack] Obama of "releasing criminals into our communities to promote his political agenda on sequestration." ("Several hundred are related to sequester," Homeland Security secretary Janet Napolitano later said, "but it wasn't thousands.") Republican senator Jeff Sessions of Alabama said the White House "further demonstrated that it has no commitment to enforcing the law and cannot be trusted to deliver on any future promises of enforcement."

DHS quickly halted plans to release an additional 3,000 low-risk detainees in March, much to the dismay of immigrant advocates and proponents of reduced government spending. The government holds roughly 30,000 undocumented people in custody on any given day, mostly in privately run prisons. It costs about $164 per inmate per day, according to one widely cited figure, versus as little as 30 cents per day to release the same individual to community supervision, where they are required to attend court hearings and, in most instances, face deportation.

"The scaling back of the detention system is something that's doable," Barón says. "It's unfortunate that it's come in the context of the sequester, but we do hope even if it came about for the wrong reasons it can lead to a discussion of whether we should be spending all that money and inflicting a lot of human damage."

Detention and deportation of undocumented immigrants costs about $5 billion per year, or roughly $12,500 for every person shipped home. Many of those currently being expelled from the country will likely qualify for permanent residency or other legal status under the leading immigration reform proposals. So why doesn't Obama simply halt deportations of all noncriminal undocumented immigrants until the proposed changes take effect?

The Use of Prosecutorial Discretion

Despite the indignant protests of conservatives, prosecutorial discretion—the tool used in the February detainee releases—is a relatively uncontested power of the executive branch. Randy Beck, Justice Thomas O. Marshall chair of constitutional law at the University of Georgia, says the president's job is to enforce the law but there is room for leniency.

"There usually is enough play in the joints of statutes to give the executive branch a subtle way of adopting regulations and enforcement priorities," Beck says. "If you sat people down and explained, 'Look, we don't have the resources to deport everybody. We have to pick and choose and we're just going to choose people who have committed serious offenses,' most people would get on board with that. Of course, that's not the way it gets reported or spun or whatever."

In 2012, when Obama signed his executive order enacting the Deferred Action for Childhood Arrivals (DACA) program, the outrage was vociferous. Commonly linked to the DREAM [Development, Relief, and Education for Alien Minors] Act, the stalled legislation it seeks to temporarily take the place of, DACA grants work authorization and a temporary reprieve from deportation to certain undocumented young people. Senator Chuck Grassley of Iowa called the decree "an affront to the process of representative government."

The tone of the immigration debate has softened considerably over the past year and even weeks, but even the bipartisan Senate push for an immigration fix seeks vaguely defined border security benchmarks that must be met before changes take effect. Last week, Senator Rand Paul proposed an annual vote by Congress to "certify" the border as secure before reforms proceed. Immigration rights advocates are concerned that deportations and detentions could be used as the standard by which security is judged.

"The administration has put itself in a little bit of a bind," Barón says. "They've been trying to say, 'We're really tough on enforcement and we're deporting a lot of people.' Now anytime they seem to be backing off that they're going to be called out. The way they should be talking about it is, 'We realize we don't need to have these people detained. It's not humane, we're working on comprehensive immigration reform. We're not dropping those cases.'"

The Constitutionality of Presidential Discretion

Whether Obama could legally expand the DACA program to include a much broader swath of the country's estimated 11 million undocumented immigrants depends on whom you ask. John Yoo, the George W. Bush administration deputy assistant attorney general whose legal memoranda justified "enhanced interrogation" techniques, blasted DACA in a law review article in September, describing it as a "breach of duty" under the Constitution.

On the other hand, Kenneth R. Mayer, a professor of political science at the University of Wisconsin and author of the book *With the Stroke of a Pen: Executive Orders and Presidential Power*, argues history is littered with executive orders popular with the president's party and condemned by the opposition.

"Democrats and liberals say, 'This is wonderful, it's about time,' while conservatives and Republicans are outraged, saying 'He's nullifying a law, he can't do that!'" Mayer says. "The answer is they're both right. In practice, the president can do this. But Congress could try to stop him, and the way they do that is raising the political cost to a degree the president doesn't find acceptable."

With immigration reform legislation inching toward the president's desk, it's unlikely he'll waste political capital by halting deportations or even reducing the immigrant detainee population, despite the budgetary considerations. The prospect of doing anything that might alienate Republicans, especially with a compromise so close, alarms activists like Tamar Jacoby, president of ImmigrationWorks USA, an advocacy group comprised largely of small business owners.

"We have a Congress for a reason," Jacoby says. "To fix anything permanently you need to have legislation, and in order for that to happen it has to be bipartisan. My worst nightmare is the president thinking, 'I don't need bipartisan legislation. Why share credit with Republicans? I can just go on and do this myself.' I think that's a disastrous political strategy."

The Political Hurdles

If the current congressional push for immigration reform were to fail, however, a presidential pardon for undocumented immigrants with no criminal history might be Obama's last ditch alternative to prosecutorial discretion. Rather than scaling back on detentions, Obama could instantly—and permanently—legalize millions of illegal immigrants. Beck, the Georgia law scholar, notes that the Constitution empowers the president to "grant reprieves and pardons for offenses against the United States, except in cases of impeachment."

The question, he says, is "whether coming into the country in violation of the immigration laws or overstaying a visa could be deemed an 'offense against the United States.'" But the president has broad powers of pardon, and it seems that Obama could exercise those powers here. Beck cites *United States v. Klein*, an 1871 Supreme Court case that involved a presidential pardon issued during the Civil War to confederates who rejoined the union and took an oath of loyalty.

But even if executive branch lawyers could put forth a legal rationale for the move, there are political reasons why

Obama would likely be reluctant to make it. Although potentially cementing loyalty from a generation of Latinos, a mass pardon would likely be deeply unpopular with moderates and liberals who put faith in the legislative process, and would be considered downright treasonous by many Republicans. Obama could face congressional censure or perhaps even impeachment if he had any time remaining in office, and the backlash against Democrats could make the Tea Party–fueled, Obamacare-inspired shellacking of 2010 look mild.

"If in December 2016 Obama says, 'Unconditional pardon to everybody in the country illegally,' that would totally dismantle Democratic Party governance for a generation," Mayer says. "I don't think he wants that to be his legacy."

> *"When you label someone an 'illegal alien' or 'illegal immigrant' or just plain 'illegal,' you are effectively saying the individual, as opposed to the actions the person has taken, is unlawful."*

Why "Illegal Immigrant" Is a Slur

Charles Garcia

In the following viewpoint, Charles Garcia argues that labeling a person illegal, whether through use of the noun or adjective, is damaging and mistaken. Garcia contends that the use of "illegal immigrant" or "illegal alien" is demeaning. Furthermore, he contends that the terminology is incorrect, as not all migrant workers residing unlawfully have committed a crime. He claims that use of the terminology is politically motivated and manipulative. Garcia is chief executive officer of Garcia Trujillo, a merchant bank dedicated to the advancement of the Hispanic community.

As you read, consider the following questions:

1. In what year and in what context was the term "illegal immigrant" first used, according to Garcia?

2. Garcia cites a study by a journalism professor finding that what percentage of news stories published between 2000 and 2010 on the issue used the terms "illegal immigrant" or "illegal alien"?

3. The author claims that hate crimes against Latinos rose in what year?

L ast month's [June 2012] Supreme Court decision in the landmark Arizona immigration case was groundbreaking for what it omitted: the words "illegal immigrants" and "illegal aliens," except when quoting other sources. The court's non-judgmental language established a humanistic approach to our current restructuring of immigration policy.

Using the Term "Illegal"

When you label someone an "illegal alien" or "illegal immigrant" or just plain "illegal," you are effectively saying the individual, as opposed to the actions the person has taken, is unlawful. The terms imply the very existence of an unauthorized migrant in America is criminal.

In this country, there is still a presumption of innocence that requires a jury to convict someone of a crime. If you don't pay your taxes, are you an illegal? What if you get a speeding ticket? A murder conviction? No. You're still not an illegal. Even alleged terrorists and child molesters aren't labeled illegals.

By becoming judge, jury and executioner, you dehumanize the individual and generate animosity toward them. *New York Times* editorial writer Lawrence Downes says "illegal" is often "a code word for racial and ethnic hatred."

The term "illegal immigrant" was first used in 1939 as a slur by the British toward Jews who were fleeing the Nazis and entering Palestine without authorization. Holocaust survivor and Nobel Peace Prize winner Elie Wiesel aptly said that "no human being is illegal."

Misconceptions About Migrant Workers

Migrant workers residing unlawfully in the U.S. are not—and never have been—criminals. They are subject to deportation, through a civil administrative procedure that differs from criminal prosecution, and where judges have wide discretion to allow certain foreign nationals to remain here.

Another misconception is that the vast majority of migrant workers currently out of status sneak across our southern border in the middle of the night. Actually, almost half enter the U.S. with a valid tourist or work visa and overstay their allotted time. Many go to school, find a job, get married and start a family. And some even join the Marine Corps, like Lance Cpl. Jose Gutierrez, who was the first combat veteran to die in the Iraq War. While he was granted American citizenship posthumously, there are another 38,000 noncitizens in uniform, including undocumented immigrants, defending our country.

Justice Anthony Kennedy, writing for the majority, joined by Chief Justice John Roberts and three other justices, stated: "As a general rule, it is not a crime for a removable alien to remain present in the United States." The court also ruled that it was not a crime to seek or engage in unauthorized employment.

As Kennedy explained, removal of an unauthorized migrant is a civil matter where even if the person is out of status, federal officials have wide discretion to determine whether deportation makes sense. For example, if an unauthorized person is trying to support his family by working or has "children born in the United States, long ties to the community, or

Being an "Illegal" Immigrant

Having crossed the border without permission does not render a person necessarily an "illegal immigrant".

You can cross the border without permission, and later obtain legalisation and even citizenship. Just as going over the speed limit once does not make you an "illegal driver", nor does crossing the border once make you an "illegal immigrant".

Tanya Golash-Boza, "No Human Being Is Illegal:
It's Time to Drop the 'I-Word,'" Al Jazeera, April 8, 2013.

a record of distinguished military service," officials may let him stay. Also, if individuals or their families might be politically persecuted or harmed upon return to their country of origin, they may also remain in the United States.

The Language Used by Journalists

While the Supreme Court has chosen language less likely to promote hatred and divisiveness, journalists continue using racially offensive language.

University of Memphis journalism professor Thomas Hrach conducted a study of 122,000 news stories published between 2000 and 2010 to determine which terms are being used to describe foreign nationals in the U.S. who are out of status. He found that 89% of the time during this period, journalists used the biased terms "illegal immigrant" and "illegal alien."

Hrach discovered that there was a substantial increase in the use of the term "illegal immigrant," which he correlated back to the *Associated Press [AP] Stylebook*'s decision in 2004 to recommend "illegal immigrant" to its members. (It's the preferred term at CNN and the *New York Times* as well.) The *AP Stylebook* is the decisive authority on word use at virtually all mainstream daily newspapers, and it's used by editors at television, radio and electronic news media. According to the AP, this term is "accurate and neutral." [Editor's note: As of April 2013, the Associated Press no longer sanctions the use of the term "illegal immigrant" to describe a person.]

For the AP to claim that "illegal immigrant" is "accurate and neutral" is like Moody's giving Bernie Madoff's hedge fund a triple-A rating for safety and creditworthiness.

The Importance of Language

It's almost as if the AP were following the script of pollster and Fox News contributor Frank Luntz, considered the foremost GOP [Republican] expert on crafting the perfect conservative political message. In 2005, he produced a 25-page secret memorandum that would radically alter the immigration debate to distort public perception of the issue.

The secret memorandum almost perfectly captures [2012 Republican presidential candidate] Mitt Romney's position on immigration—along with that of every anti-immigrant politician and conservative pundit. For maximum impact, Luntz urges Republicans to offer fearful rhetoric: "This is about overcrowding of YOUR schools, emergency room chaos in YOUR hospitals, the increase in YOUR taxes, and the crime in YOUR communities." He also encourages them to talk about "border security," because after 9/11 [referring to the September 11, 2001, terrorist attacks on the United States], this "argument does well among all voters—even hard-core Democrats," as it conjures up the specter of terrorism.

George Orwell's classic *Nineteen Eighty-Four* shows how even a free society is susceptible to manipulation by overdosing on worn-out prefabricated phrases that convert people into lifeless dummies, who become easy prey for the political class.

In *Nineteen Eighty-Four*, Orwell creates a character named Syme who I find eerily similar to Luntz. Syme is a fast-talking word genius in the research department of the Ministry of Truth. He invents doublespeak for Big Brother and edits the Newspeak Dictionary by destroying words that might lead to "thoughtcrimes." Section B contains the doublespeak words with political implications that will spread in speakers' minds like a poison.

In Luntz's book *Words That Work*, Appendix B lists "The 21 Political Words and Phrases You Should Never Say Again." For example, destroy "undocumented worker" and instead say "illegal immigrant," because "the label" you use "determines the attitudes people have toward them."

And the poison is effective. Surely it's no coincidence that in 2010, hate crimes against Latinos made up 66% of the violence based on ethnicity, up from 45% in 2009, according to the FBI [Federal Bureau of Investigation].

In his essay "Politics and the English Language," Orwell warned that one must be constantly on guard against a ready-made phrase that "anaesthetizes a portion of one's brain." But Orwell also wrote that "from time to time one can even, if one jeers loudly enough, send some worn-out and useless phrase . . . into the dustbin, where it belongs"—just like the U.S. Supreme Court did.

> "The legally accurate term for those in the United States illegally is 'illegal alien.'"

The Accurate Term Should Be "Illegal Alien"

Jon Feere

In the following viewpoint, Jon Feere argues that the move by the Associated Press and other journalists to change the terminology in referring to those in the United States illegally is legally inaccurate. Feere contends that anyone who is not an American citizen but is in America is an alien under the law. Furthermore, he contends that there are aliens who are legal aliens and those who are illegal aliens. He claims that the term "immigrant" should only be used when a person is in the process of becoming a permanent American resident or citizen. Feere is a legal policy analyst at the Center for Immigration Studies.

As you read, consider the following questions:

1. Who does the author say is trying to get journalists to embrace what he calls activist terminology?

2. What document does the author say a person should have in order to be properly called an immigrant?

3. Feere accuses the newspaper industry of shifting from using the term "illegal alien" to using what?

In a victory for those who want to further blur the line between legal and illegal, the Associated Press [AP] has announced its decision to stop using the term "illegal immigrant" in its articles. Instead, the new "acceptable variations" include "living in or entering a country illegally" or "without legal permission." Journalists make it a rule to be concise and not wordy. But such standards are thrown out the window when it comes to the illegal immigration issue, it seems.

The Legally Accurate Term

The legally accurate term for those in the United States illegally is "illegal alien." Prior to today's [April 2, 2013] decision, the AP supported use of the term "illegal immigrant." But even that term represented a move away from accurate language. This language trend is part of a concerted effort by immigration groups and amnesty advocates that seeks to get journalists to embrace activist terminology. This effort also rears its head every time a journalist uses a euphemism for amnesty (e.g., "normalization of status").

Last year, I analyzed language used in the immigration debate and attempted to highlight some of the arguments made by advocates of activist terminology. One such activist was linguist Jennifer Sclafani who, when asked by the *American Journalism Review* whether it makes a difference to use the term "illegal alien" as opposed to "illegal immigrant," responded, "Yes, absolutely it does. No matter which way you look at it, an alien is always an outsider."

And that is the correct way of looking at immigration. Those who are here on tourist visas, for example, are legal aliens. Those who entered illegally are illegal aliens. In both instances, they are aliens—i.e., "outsiders"—who are not part of the American citizenry. This is a basic legal and logical fact. The word "immigrant" should be reserved for those who—as defined by Merriam-Webster—come to a country for "permanent residence." In other words, the term "legal immigrant" or "immigrant" should only be used where the individual is entering the United States on a permanent basis and has received a green card. In fact, the official USCIS [U.S. Citizenship and Immigration Services] glossary defines "immigrant" as someone who has been "admitted to the United States as a lawful permanent resident." If he later acquires U.S. citizenship, he becomes a citizen and is no longer an immigrant. This makes the term "illegal immigrant" somewhat self-contradictory.

A Shift in Language

Despite the term's problems, the Associated Press defended use of the term "illegal immigrant" as recently as October of last year. To its credit, the news-gathering outlet pushed back against activist groups and also ruled out use of the term "undocumented." But only a few months later, the AP has dropped even "illegal immigrant."

The AP explains that the change is justified because it is "ridding the *Stylebook* of labels," noting that instead of referring to someone as a schizophrenic, they refer to a person as someone "diagnosed with schizophrenia." And since they now plan to label behavior rather than people, as they put it, the term "illegal immigrant" must go. One wonders whether this logic will also apply to the thieves, adulterers, and murderers who become the subject of an AP article. No longer will we read reports of murderers; instead, expect to see "persons engaged in an act that unlawfully ends the life of another."

It's unclear how far this trend will go. In another piece from last year, I highlighted an e-mail exchange I had with editors at two California newspapers that referred to illegal aliens as "undocumented Californians." Of course one does not acquire a state's citizenship simply by entering the state. A U.S. citizen from Nevada who visits San Francisco does not automatically become a Californian, nor does a citizen from Mexico who crosses the national border into San Diego. But this was just the start. In February of this year, the *San Francisco Chronicle* referred to an illegal alien from South Korea as "one of an estimated 2.1 million *American* youths" who might be eligible for deferred action. According to some journalists, illegal aliens are already Americans. I sent the *Chronicle* a few inquiries about this description (and a separate error in the article), but the writers have refused to respond to my e-mails.

The point is, when it comes to language in the immigration debate, the newspaper industry seems to be slowly shifting from the term "illegal alien" to "American."

Periodical and Internet Sources Bibliography

The following articles have been selected to supplement the diverse views presented in this chapter.

Steve Chapman	"Illegal Immigrants, Not So Illegal," *Chicago Tribune*, August 19, 2012.
Elizabeth Dwoskin	"Why Letting Illegal Immigrants Out of Jail Makes Sense," *Bloomberg Businessweek*, March 5, 2013.
Jon Feere	"Is the 'Kids Act' Amnesty Really Just for Kids? Probably Not," Center for Immigration Studies, February 2014.
Tanya Golash-Boza	"No Human Being Is Illegal: It's Time to Drop the 'I-Word,'" Al Jazeera, April 8, 2013.
Ed Morales	"Stop Using 'Illegal' to Describe Undocumented Immigrants," *Progressive*, October 10, 2012.
Ruben Navarrette Jr.	"'Illegal Immigrant' Is the Uncomfortable Truth," CNN, July 6, 2012.
Peter Skerry	"No Kidding: Republicans, Democrats, and Illegal Immigrants," *Weekly Standard*, August 12, 2013.
Andrew Stiles	"The Deportation Lie," *National Review Online*, April 19, 2013.
Andrew Stiles	"The Kids Act's Risks" *National Review Online*, August 19, 2013.
Cesar Vargas	"Don't End My American DREAM," *Politico*, July 23, 2013.
Jessica M. Vaughan	"Where Are All the Deportations?," *Washington Times*, December 29, 2013.

OPPOSING
VIEWPOINTS®
SERIES

CHAPTER 4

How Should US Immigration Policy Be Reformed?

Chapter Preface

The issue of how the United States should reform current policy on immigration is rife with controversy. There are two main questions at hand: 1) What policies should address the almost twelve million unauthorized immigrants currently in the United States? and 2) What should be done about illegal immigration in the future? The proposed answers to these questions are invariably influenced by the way the United States dealt with similar issues in 1986.

The Immigration Reform and Control Act (IRCA), also known as the Simpson-Mazzoli Act, was passed by Congress and signed into law by President Ronald Reagan in 1986. IRCA reformed United States immigration law in order to control illegal immigration. With respect to the control of future illegal immigration, it attempted to halt illegal immigration by enacting sanctions for employers who knowingly hire unauthorized immigrants and requiring employers to attest to their employees' legal immigration status. It also attempted to meet the needs of employers by legalizing certain seasonal agricultural workers. With respect to unauthorized immigrants residing in the United States at that time, IRCA allowed a process whereby legal permanent residence could be obtained, with a path to citizenship possible.

This last component of IRCA has been the most controversial. The so-called amnesty of illegal immigrants was intended to be a onetime occurrence, and the other components of the law were to prevent further illegal immigration. At the time of IRCA, it was estimated that there were five million unauthorized immigrants in the United States. A little over half of them took advantage of the amnesty option, obtaining legal status. The rest either did not qualify or did not enroll in the program. IRCA on the whole, however, did not halt illegal immigration; over twenty-five years later, there are more than eleven million unauthorized immigrants in the United States, more than double the amount that existed at the time that IRCA was passed.

As the authors of the viewpoints in this chapter illustrate, competing arguments exist on the issue of immigration reform in the United States. Some say that IRCA is evidence that amnesty is a failed policy. David S. Addington, in a Heritage Foundation *Backgrounder*, writes, "Grants of amnesty, regardless of the form of the reward they give to aliens who knowingly entered or remain in the US, discourage respect for the law, treat law-breaking aliens better than law-following aliens, and encourage future unlawful immigration into the United States." However, others claim that the amnesty in 1986 was not what caused further illegal immigration. Philip E. Wolgin and Abhay Aneja at the Center for American Progress argue, "The central reason IRCA never stood a chance at stopping unauthorized migration was that it failed to acknowledge and regulate the integrated North American labor market that already existed. It did not look to the future or create new legal channels for economic migrants." What is clear is that one's opinion about the 1986 reforms affects one's views on current immigration initiatives.

> *"Once the enforcement agenda ... has been completed, which is likely to take several years, amnesty would be a risk worth taking."*

Enforcement, Then Amnesty, on Immigration

Mark Krikorian

In the following viewpoint, Mark Krikorian argues that before illegal immigrants should be given legal status through amnesty, the border must be secured, new hires must be subjected to E-Verify, and existing laws must be enforced. He argues that amnesty should only be given to noncriminals, and that after amnesty, legal immigration should be cut to offset the amnesty. Krikorian is the executive director of the Center for Immigration Studies.

As you read, consider the following questions:

1. What was wrong with the 1986 amnesty, according to Krikorian?

2. Under the guidelines Krikorian establishes, approximately how many illegal immigrants would qualify for amnesty?

3. After amnesty, Krikorian argues that legal immigration should be cut to how many people annually?

President Obama's State of the Union address all but ignored immigration, so as not to further complicate Speaker [John] Boehner's efforts to get the House GOP to pass an amnesty and increases in immigration. In furtherance of those efforts, House Republicans will discuss immigration this afternoon at their annual retreat on Maryland's eastern shore. The session will be held behind closed doors and can be expected to be contentious, given the growing resistance among Republican lawmakers to handing a major political victory to a president wounded by the Obamacare fiasco. But we already know the basic outline of the immigration principles to be put forth by the party leadership, and they're what anyone might have guessed: enhanced border security and interior enforcement, systems for verifying workers and tracking legal entrants, visa-program reforms, and a path to legal status for current illegal immigrants.

The [Charles] Schumer–[Marco] Rubio amnesty bill passed in June by the Senate would bring about all these things, at least nominally. House members' protestations that they reject the Senate bill mean nothing if the House simply proposes to pass all the Senate bill's constituent parts in separately numbered measures. This is what President Obama and other amnesty supporters mean when they express support for the House's piecemeal or "step by step" approach.

The release of their principles for reform clearly suggests that Boehner, [Eric] Cantor, and the rest of the Republican leadership are going to try to trick their members and supporters into permitting passage of something like the Senate bill. With Obama as chief executive and Harry Reid as Senate majority leader, the only defensible reaction from conservatives is "No": no bill that empowers Obama to amnesty illegals, however strong the enforcement promises might be, since they will be ignored. But while "No" is the necessary short-term answer, conservatives also need a plan to manage the transition from our current unsettled politics of immigration to a more stable and sustainable situation.

The basic outline would be this: enforcement first, without preconditions or trade-offs, but targeted mainly at the prevention of new illegal immigration. Once that's fully in place, we can move on to the grand bargain: amnesty for remaining long-established, nonviolent illegals in exchange for an end to mass legal immigration.

Proponents of amnesty say that the demand for "enforcement first" is a ruse, and that immigration hawks keep moving the goalposts as a way of avoiding amnesty. There are no doubt some amnesty opponents who fit that description, but the broad accusation ignores the fact that basic, decades-old demands regarding enforcement, such as for the implementation of employment-verification and exit-tracking systems, still have not been satisfied. The public has good reason not to believe promises of future enforcement, having heard them all before.

The Schumer-Rubio attempt to reduce this mistrust by amnestying illegals up front but making their upgrade to full green-card status contingent on future enforcement benchmarks is a fraud. None of the amnestied illegals, however "provisional" their status is said to be, would ever revert to illegal status, whether or not the enforcement goals were met. (In the past, groups who have been granted temporary status have routinely had it extended, and there will be tremendous political pressure to treat the current illegal population similarly.) And once that population has legal status, immigration hawks lose the only leverage they have: No pro-amnesty official, Republican or Democrat, who now professes his undying support for future enforcement will have any incentive to follow through at that point.

Immigration reform skeptics trusted lawmakers in 1986 and got burned: Amnesty was granted, but enforcement did not happen. This time, *they're* going to have to trust *us*. Once the first part of this new deal is in place (the necessary enforcement tools), there will still be significant political pressure to follow through with the second part (amnesty plus immigration curbs). In this it differs from the amnesty-before-enforcement approach of 1986, which is also the basis of the Senate bill.

At the same time, any enforcement arrangement that throws millions of illegal aliens out of work all at once (as certain enforcement tools would do) would be unacceptable to the public, not to mention un-Burkean. For that reason, the enforcement efforts that must precede any discussion of amnesty should focus chiefly on preventing, and punishing, *new* illegal settlement. This would still induce significant numbers of illegal immigrants, mainly more recent arrivals with fewer attachments here, to return voluntarily to their country of origin, by, for example, making it more difficult for them to seek new jobs.

That doesn't mean that no illegals already here would be deported or encouraged to leave. In fact, because of the Secure Communities program (which checks the fingerprints of arrestees against Department of Homeland Security databases, as well as those of the FBI), Immigration and Customs Enforcement [ICE] is aware of a much larger number of illegal-alien criminals than ever before, which means deportations should be increasing. Instead, overall "removals" dropped 10 percent last year, and genuine deportations (of illegals in the interior of the country rather than those caught at the border) have declined 40 percent since 2009. Right now, because of policies euphemistically called "prosecutorial discretion," ICE is releasing more illegal-alien criminals than it is deporting.

To restore public confidence that the government is serious about enforcement, ICE agents should be given discretion to do their job, and local police and sheriffs ought to be allowed to help them, especially in cases that affect public safety. As it stands now, directives from ICE management instruct agents not to take action against illegal immigrants in many cases, even when they have been apprehended by local law enforcement for other reasons.

Nonetheless, the procedures that most need to be put in place would focus mainly on new illegals. For instance, making E-Verify a universal part of the hiring process—to make it hard for illegal aliens to get jobs—would not affect illegal aliens already in jobs, since it would be used only for new hires (although it's true that established illegals who leave their current jobs would have trouble finding new ones).

The same focus on new illegals would apply in visa tracking. Since 1996, Congress on eight separate occasions has mandated the creation of an electronic system to track the entry and exit of foreign visitors, and we still don't have one. Such a system is essential for immigration control, since between one-third and one-half of the 12 million current illegal aliens entered the country legally—as tourists, students, business travelers, etc.—but never left. Granting any sort of legal status to yesterday's visa overstayers before ensuring that new visitors can't overstay is absurd.

The executive must also show a good-faith commitment to muscular, unapologetic enforcement of immigration laws going forward. Our experience since the 1986 amnesty shows that this is necessary regardless of the party in power. Among such confidence-building measures would be criminal prosecution of every new border infiltrator and every new visa overstayer. Border prosecutions are already under way in certain limited areas, but with apprehensions down 70 percent from 2005, it is now practical to adopt a zero-tolerance strategy along the entire border. Congress would have to make overstaying a visa a criminal offense like border-jumping (it's now simply a civil infraction), but in both cases the goal is not to stuff the prisons with illegal aliens but rather to send the message that this time, we mean business.

We haven't yet mentioned building more border fencing or hiring more Border Patrol agents. Both of those changes are probably called for—only about 2 percent of the border has double fencing, and the Border Patrol, though bigger than it used to be, has to keep an eye on 8,000 miles of frontier with fewer officers than the New York police department. But the border is better controlled nowadays, largely because beefing up border security has been politically easier than other enforcement priorities.

Even though they focus on preventing new illegal settlement, these measures would result in significant attrition of the current illegal population. The Pew Research Center's Hispanic Trends Project has estimated that from 2005 to 2010, 1.4 million Mexicans (or "Mexicans," since 20 percent were U.S.-born children) left the United States. Some of this migration was due to the recession, some to grudging increases in enforcement late in the Bush administration, and some to the many other reasons a person might return home from abroad—retirement, injury, homesickness, the desire to protect children from the gang culture of the *barrio*. Unfortunately, during that same period 1.4 million *new* Mexicans entered the U.S. (most of them illegally), resulting in net migration of roughly zero. The slightly better economy and Obama's gutting of enforcement have caused the number of illegal immigrants to start increasing again, but the recent churn in the illegal population suggests that even measures devoted mainly to preventing new immigration can result in a shrinkage of the existing illegal population. For example, one study found that implementation of Arizona's 2007 E-Verify law caused the illegal working-age population in the state to fall by 17 percent in one year.

The enforcement measures we have discussed are not sufficient. While their full implementation would establish a new approach to immigration management, additional changes would need to be included in any future immigration grand bargain in order to identify and remove future illegal immigrants, as well as those who are already here but don't qualify for amnesty. Such additional measures would include retroactive application of E-Verify to non-amnestied illegals, and institutionalized cooperation between ICE, IRS [Interval Revenue Service], and the Social Security Administration [SSA] to locate and apprehend identity thieves, including new offices within the SSA and the IRS specifically devoted to identifying illegal aliens for ICE.

Finally, any future deal would have to include an end to the anachronistic practice of automatically conferring citizenship on children born to foreign tourists, foreign students, and illegal aliens. Automatic citizenship at birth should be restricted to children of citizens or permanent residents (with, perhaps, a sort of statute of limitations as in Australia, where a child born to illegals can become a citizen if he spends his entire first ten years in the country).

All this having been fully implemented and any legal challenges overcome, what's the next step? The enforcement-first or attrition-through-enforcement approach lays the groundwork for a legislative bargain that would, one hopes, establish a new equilibrium. Such a package would include, in addition to the last pieces of enforcement mentioned above, amnesty for established illegals in exchange for a more moderate level of legal immigration in the future.

Amnesty is, of course, the most controversial part of any immigration plan. It rewards liars and scofflaws. It mocks those who obeyed the law. It permits illegal immigrants to keep positions that could be filled by Americans looking for full-time work. It creates large future costs for taxpayers. It can serve as a catalyst for future illegal and chain immigration. It is likely to be plagued by significant fraud.

Nevertheless, once the enforcement agenda outlined above has been completed, which is likely to take several years, amnesty would be a risk worth taking. And the combination of a new enforcement paradigm plus reduced legal immigration would address many (though not all) of the potential problems with it.

First, a word about terminology. In the immigration context, an amnesty is anything that permits illegal aliens to remain legally. In other words, legalization *is* amnesty. Politicians and activists have obfuscated this point for years in an attempt to deceive voters. In 2000, the National Council of La Raza did focus-group testing in preparation for the anticipated Bush amnesty push and advised the Mexican and American governments to avoid the word "amnesty" at all costs because people disliked it so much. Any politician arguing that his legalization plan du jour is not really an amnesty simply cannot be trusted. If we're going to let some illegal aliens stay, let us call it amnesty.

Who should benefit from such an amnesty? The bulk should be people without criminal convictions who have U.S.-born children or U.S.-citizen or legal-resident spouses, plus those who came before age ten and have grown up here. Recent estimates suggest that as of three years ago, there were 4.4 million illegal aliens with U.S.-born children, and perhaps 600,000 with citizen or legal-resident spouses (but without U.S.-born children). Add to that adult illegals who came here before age ten, who might number another 500,000, plus the illegal-alien spouses and minor children of these various groups, and you're at perhaps 6 million people, or half the current illegal population of about 12 million (though the total will have shrunk somewhat before the amnesty owing to deportation, voluntary departure, or death).

In addition, it would be prudent, given their long residence, to amnesty those who've lived here for more than a decade but don't qualify under other categories. DHS estimated that as of three years ago, about 10 million of the 12 million illegal aliens had entered before 2004. Even a relatively lenient amnesty, however, would exclude a significant number of people for criminality, gang membership, and other reasons; the Congressional Budget Office has estimated that 30 percent of the illegal population would not receive amnesty under the terms of the Schumer-Rubio bill for these reasons.

It would be fair to estimate, then, that out of an illegal population shrunk by attrition to 10 million people, some 6 or 7 million would qualify for amnesty.

The form of the amnesty should be relatively straightforward. Fees should be modest; requirements should be few and clear, but scrupulously enforced (by an immigration bureaucracy that is given sufficient time and resources to do the job properly). Amnesty beneficiaries should get green cards—i.e., become regular legal immigrants who can, if they qualify, become citizens (though if the experience of the 1986 amnesty is any indication, a large share will choose not to pursue citizenship).

Requirements in other amnesty proposals, including the Schumer-Rubio bill, for large fines or permanent noncitizen status are punitive window dressing, designed exclusively to help get legislation passed. The fines will be waived, the permanent noncitizen status upgraded to full green cards after a few years. The real goal should in any case not be punishment but confession and absolution. All amnesty beneficiaries should have to participate in public ceremonies where they read aloud a confession (preferably in their native tongue) along the lines of: "I acknowledge that I showed disrespect to America's laws and have no right to remain in the United States. But having put down roots here, I humbly ask the American people to forgive my trespasses and accept me as a legal resident of their country. If accepted, I will strive to be worthy of this generosity, so help me God." Such a secular sacrament of confession should close the book on their illegal status.

The corollary to amnestying certain illegal aliens is that all those who do not qualify must be removed. No amnesty applicant should be notified by mail as to the disposition of his case; rather, he must appear in person, and if rejected, immediately be taken into custody and sent home. Any encounter with the authorities, no matter how minor, that reveals the illegal status of one of the much-reduced number of remaining (or new) illegals must result in deportation. Amnesty can be justified only as a transition to meticulous and aggressive enforcement.

The other half of the bargain is reduced future immigration. This is the precise opposite of current proposals. When the House GOP leadership talks of "reforms to visa programs," what it means is increases in "temporary" worker programs for farmers, tech companies, and other special interests. The Schumer-Rubio bill would double legal immigration and nearly double admissions of guest workers.

Such increases are essentially pork-barrel measures; businesses get cheap, controllable labor, and ethnic-chauvinist groups get a never-ending supply of people through family immigration that they can claim to speak for. But the principled argument offered for these huge increases in legal immigration is that they're the only way to end illegal immigration. Advocates claim that there's nothing that can be done to stop foreigners from moving here, so by letting in everyone who wants to come, we—by definition—no longer have to worry about illegal immigration. As New York University professor Jorge Castañeda put it to me during a recent television appearance, we must not only amnesty past immigrants but *future* ones as well.

If you accept the premise that immigration control is impossible, then numerical or category limits are indeed irrelevant. But if you accept that immigration can be controlled, then it's necessary to decide whom and how many to admit. We currently take in 1.1 million legal immigrants each year, the large majority simply because they have relatives here. This number should be reduced, for several reasons.

Most immediately, cuts to legal immigration are called for to offset the amnesty. Cutting immigration in half, to roughly 500,000 a year, would mean it would take twelve years to offset the legalization of 6 million illegal aliens. Offsets like this have been used in immigration law before; the unskilled worker category was reduced in 1997 for as long as it took to offset an amnesty for various Central American illegal aliens.

But a simple offset concedes that the existing immigration level of 1 million plus per year is acceptable. On the contrary, high levels of legal immigration in themselves create high levels of illegal immigration. The two figures have risen together, and for immigrants from the same countries, because legal immigration creates the networks and connections that make illegal immigration possible. What's more, in our system a huge number of relatives of immigrants qualify on paper to immigrate but are put on waiting lists because of numerical caps in various immigration categories; many of them just come anyway and wait for their number to come up. This is especially important in the wake of an amnesty. It's bad enough to have rewarded illegal aliens, but to reward their *relatives* with legal-immigration slots is galling and indefensible.

The more fundamental problem with mass legal immigration, however, is that it's an anachronism, something we've outgrown. As a young nation settling the land and later industrializing, we could successfully make use of a large number of new workers from abroad, though even in the past immigration created great social turmoil. But we are today a very different, more mature, nation. Our post-industrial, knowledge-based economy offers fewer opportunities for advancement to legal newcomers with little education, at the same time that our own less educated are under great stress. A modern welfare state means that less skilled legal workers, who necessarily earn low wages, create huge costs to taxpayers. Modern transportation and communications, combined with a post-national American elite, mean that immigrants—even skilled immigrants—have less need to assimilate and join the American people emotionally rather than just on paper. In short, mass immigration is incompatible with contemporary society.

Many of the concerns people express regarding illegal immigration are actually about immigration as a whole, most of which is legal. Most illegal immigrants work on the books for more than minimum wage—so job competition faced by less skilled Americans has less to do with legal status and more to do with simple numbers. Likewise with welfare; illegals collect benefits on behalf of their U.S.-born children but are ineligible themselves, whereas legal immigrants use a much wider array of taxpayer-funded services. The same dynamic is true with the increase in poverty, in economic inequality, in the growth in the uninsured—legal immigration has a much larger impact than illegal.

A lower level of overall immigration would tighten the labor market, ease pressure on welfare and the health and education systems, and promote assimilation—goals that are all important in themselves, but especially important to the absorption of the amnestied illegal population. In addition to the benefits to the country, curbing immigration would help the political prospects of conservatism, given the mountain of data showing that immigrants are overwhelmingly big-government liberals.

To summarize, in exchange for amnesty, the following legal-immigration reforms—which together would cut legal immigration by about one-half—are called for: Family immigration should be limited to the spouses and unmarried minor children of U.S. citizens; skilled immigration should be limited to the top talent in the world; humanitarian immigration—refugees and asylum seekers—should be limited to the truly desperate who have nowhere else to go, as is not the case with the bulk of the current flow; the visa lottery should be ended; and guest-worker programs should be eliminated— they not only exploit workers and undercut Americans, but are vehicles of illegal immigration, as the Congressional Budget Office report on the Senate bill acknowledged.

If House Republicans want to offer a choice rather than an echo, they'd do well to consider the alternative to the Senate plan sketched here: enforcement first, followed by a combination of amnesty and greatly reduced immigration.

> *"Only a legislative overhaul that provides a pathway to legal status for the millions of undocumented immigrants . . . can align our enforcement policies with our national economic and social interests."*

Illegal Immigrants Should Be Put on a Path to Earned Citizenship

Marshall Fitz

In the following viewpoint, Marshall Fitz argues that although two new immigration policies are positive steps, there needs to be a pathway to citizenship for the illegal immigrants currently living in the United States. Fitz contends that the new detainer policy, regarding detention and deportation, and the new family-unity rule treat symptoms of the larger problem, which is the more than eleven million undocumented immigrants living without legal status. Fitz is director of immigration policy at the Center for American Progress.

As you read, consider the following questions:

1. According to the author, how many illegal immigrants were deported in fiscal year 2012?

2. When did the family-unity rule take effect, according to Fitz?

3. How much money did the US government spend in fiscal year 2012 on the two agencies responsible for immigration enforcement?

In the past two weeks [December 2012–January 2013], the U.S. Department of Homeland Security announced two welcome immigration policy developments: limiting what category of people should be detained under federal law and shortening the time that close family members would have to be separated when applying for legal permanent resident status. But the department also released one deeply troubling set of immigration enforcement statistics showing that more than 400,000 immigrants were deported in FY 2012. Considered together, these developments highlight the incoherence in current national immigration policy and illustrate the need for a permanent fix for our nation's immigration system—namely, creating a pathway to earned citizenship for the 11 million undocumented immigrants living here.

The New Detainer Policy

Immigration and Customs Enforcement, one of the key law enforcement agencies charged with enforcing immigration law, announced on December 21 that it would no longer issue a "detainer" request to local police to hold someone identified as potentially undocumented unless that person has been charged with a serious crime or convicted of multiple misdemeanors. The announcement aligns with the agency's evolving effort to apply so-called prosecutorial discretion: prioritizing criminals rather than long-settled and hardworking immigrants for detention and deportation.

The need for this policy has become especially acute given the broad and rapid expansion of the agency's Secure Communities program over the past four years. This program requires local police to check the immigration status of everyone arrested, even for the most minor infractions. Despite its reassuring name, the implementation of the Secure Communities program has actually undermined the sense of security in many communities, which has necessitated the corrections contained in this new detainer policy. By effectively empowering local police to trigger the deportation of an immigrant for nothing more than a minor traffic offense, the Secure Communities program has created a perception among immigrants—including legal permanent residents and naturalized citizens—that local police are de facto immigration agents. In some places, police have abused this power by racially profiling individuals who appear foreign and making pretextual arrests, thereby giving proof to the claim that "driving while brown" is a crime in some jurisdictions.

Even in places where local enforcement practices are not intentionally pernicious, the Secure Communities program and federal and local immigration collaboration have caused immigrants to distrust and fear local police. That distrust makes all residents less safe by undermining community-policing policies that depend on the entire public's cooperation such as reporting crimes and coming forward as witnesses. The long-overdue announcement that the Secure Communities program will no longer allow local police to use low-level arrests as a basis for initiating deportation proceedings should help restore the confidence and trust of immigrant communities in their police forces.

Importantly, this new policy should also help diminish the potential harm from the "papers please" provisions in effect in places such as Arizona through S.B. 1070 and Alabama through H.B. 56. Police in these states are allowed to ask anyone who they have a reasonable suspicion of being without

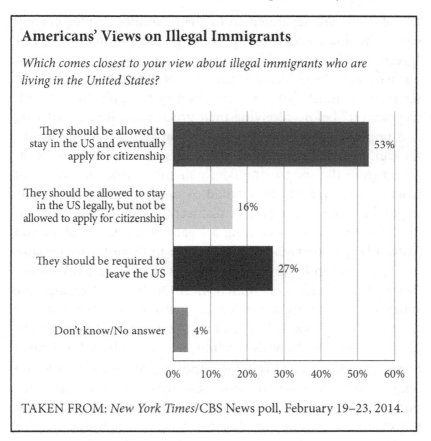

Americans' Views on Illegal Immigrants

Which comes closest to your view about illegal immigrants who are living in the United States?

They should be allowed to stay in the US and eventually apply for citizenship — 53%

They should be allowed to stay in the US legally, but not be allowed to apply for citizenship — 16%

They should be required to leave the US — 27%

Don't know/No answer — 4%

TAKEN FROM: *New York Times*/CBS News poll, February 19–23, 2014.

immigration status for proof of legality. As the Supreme Court indicated in its landmark decision in June 2012 striking down much of Arizona's law, however, it is up to the federal government to decide whether it will act on that information. The federal government has since said it will not act unless the person has been arrested for a serious offense or has been convicted of a number of offenses.

The New Family-Unity Rule

On the heels of Immigration and Customs Enforcement's refined detainer policy, U.S. [Citizenship] and Immigration Services, the agency that deals with immigration to the United States, published a final rule that will reduce the amount of time that immediate relatives (spouses and minor children) of

U.S. citizens are separated from their families. Under current law, individuals who are eligible to get an immigrant visa or "green card" because their spouse or parent is a U.S. citizen, but who have been in the United States illegally for more than six months, must first leave the country to apply for a "hardship waiver" before receiving their green card. Because of long and unpredictable processing times, having to leave the country can, in many cases, lead to months or even years of separation from the sponsoring family member. Uncertainty about whether a waiver will be granted or even how long the family might be separated acts as a disincentive for people to complete the process of becoming a legal permanent resident and instead keeps otherwise eligible people in unauthorized status.

This new family-unity rule, which was announced Wednesday and takes effect on March 4, 2013, does not change the standards or requirements for U.S. citizens seeking visas for their family members. But it allows qualified applicants to apply and wait for the waiver while they are still in the United States instead of leaving first, removing the uncertainty and long separation times. In short, the new rule is another important step toward commonsense immigration policies that reflect the realities of mixed-status American families.

The new detainer policy and the family-unity rule are smart initiatives that should be applauded, but they are treating symptoms of the problem rather than root causes. The [Barack] Obama administration has had to adopt these new policies because our dysfunctional immigration system has led to more than 11 million undocumented immigrants living in the United States, two-thirds of whom have been here for more than a decade and live in families with spouses, children, and parents who are U.S. citizens.

The Immigration Paradox

Year after year, rather than dealing realistically with the undocumented population, Congress has ordered the construction of a behemoth enforcement agency under the delusional belief that we could enforce our way to a workable system. President Barack Obama inherited this enforcement machine, and he is now on the hook for having deported 1.5 million additional immigrants, including a total of 409,849 in fiscal year 2012—the highest number of immigrants ever removed from the United States in a single year.

To be sure, everyone will agree that some of the individuals who were deported should have been deported. The Department of Homeland Security notes that among their ranks were some truly dangerous criminals, including 1,215 people convicted of homicide, 5,557 people convicted of sexual offenses, and 40,448 people convicted of drug-related crimes. But there were also hundreds of thousands of people who have not committed any crime other than the civil offense of being in the country without legal status. These are the very people whom the president has rightly argued should be provided an opportunity to earn legal status and eventually citizenship.

Herein lies the president's immigration paradox: His constitutional role as chief enforcer of federal laws flies directly in the face of what he believes those laws should provide. The recently announced initiatives reflect an effort by the administration to minimize this incoherence between practice and principle, as do prior actions such as the courageous Deferred Action for Childhood Arrivals directive, which used inherent executive authority to explicitly protect DREAM [Development, Relief, and Education for Alien Minors] Act–eligible youth, undocumented immigrants who are Americans in every way but their papers, from deportation.

The Need for Reform

Still, the senseless human toll and economic harm resulting from the continued expansion of immigration enforcement without a corresponding change in the laws cannot be corrected by administrative policy alone, and it can no longer be defended merely by reference to the rule of law. Here are three basic reasons why Congress must pass comprehensive reform.

1. *Families matter.* Permanently separating family members simply because of a lack of immigration status—without, for example, an actual criminal conviction—is un-American. As Seth Freed Wessler has estimated, more than 200,000 parents of children who are U.S. citizens were deported between 2010 and 2012. This accounted for nearly 23 percent of all deportations. Of the roughly 400,000 people deported in 2011, more than half of them were not criminals.

2. *Workers matter.* All workers suffer when an underground labor market is allowed to worsen wages and working conditions. Bringing undocumented workers off the economic sidelines and into the legal fold raises working standards and increases economic growth and productivity. This is reflected in a broad range of research from progressive and conservative think tanks, as well as from government agencies.

3. *Taxpayer dollars matter.* Finally, it is fiscally counterproductive and irrational to spend literally billions of dollars attempting to deport people who have committed no crimes, who are otherwise contributing to America's prosperity, and who would contribute more if provided legal status. The government, however, spent a total of $17.1 billion on Immigration and Customs Enforcement and Customs and Border [Protection], the two agencies charged with immigration enforcement, in FY 2012.

The decision to draw a brighter line between federal authorities and local police officers in the enforcement of immigration law, coupled with the posting of a final rule that will help families comply with the law without unnecessary separation, shows that the Obama administration is trying to rationalize a rigid and flawed immigration system. But only a legislative overhaul that provides a pathway to legal status for the millions of undocumented immigrants—already Americans in everything but paperwork—can align our enforcement policies with our national economic and social interests. If Congress were to legalize these millions of individuals, it would grow the economy, promote family stability, and save taxpayer dollars.

| "*Americans would greatly benefit from expanded immigration.*"

Immigration Benefits the United States

Doug Bandow

In the following viewpoint, Doug Bandow argues that the current immigration system needs reform. He claims that in dealing with illegal immigrants, there is an alternative in between the extremes of deportation and offering citizenship; Bandow supports the free movement of labor without necessarily offering a path to citizenship. He contends that this reform to the system, along with eliminating birthright citizenship in every case, would be politically difficult, but ultimately would allow the United States to benefit from immigration. Bandow is a senior fellow at the Cato Institute, specializing in foreign policy and civil liberties.

As you read, consider the following questions:

1. Bandow suggests that to move forward on immigration reform, Congress needs to separate what two issues?

2. According to the author, what fraction of Mexican immigrants who are eligible for citizenship have not pursued it?

3. Bandow contends that the only other developed nation to offer birthright citizenship is what country?

Immigration reform, once the top priority coming out of the 2012 presidential election, has stalled. The Senate has passed legislation, but the House is badly divided.

The Current Immigration System

The current system is a shambles. Legal categories and subcategories, quotas, and lotteries have created a flourishing legal industry. The immigration bureaucracy is a lower level of Dante's Hell. Foreign students are turned away from U.S. universities, highly skilled individuals are barred from working in America, and even political refugees sometimes are denied entry.

Finally, some 11 million people live in the U.S. illegally. They invest less in America, are vulnerable to abuse, and disrupt an already incomprehensible immigration policy.

Attempting to fence off the country is no answer to anything. It would be difficult for a generally free society with extensive borders to close out the rest of the world. Worse, to be effective, such controls as ID cards, citizenship checks, workplace raids, employer sanctions, and more would undermine domestic liberties.

The Benefits of Immigration

Anyway, immigration benefits the U.S. The economic advantages are significant. Many immigrants are natural entrepreneurs, establishing companies, creating jobs, and driving innovation. Well-educated and highly trained foreign workers are inventive and productive. Expanded workforces increase business flexibility, allowing companies to quickly respond to changing demands. Larger labor forces also encourage specialization. Labor productivity rises as companies adjust to larger workforces and invest in employees.

Immigration may depress wages for the least skilled workers. However, these are the last jobs that government should seek to protect. Moreover, the workforce, like the economy, is not a fixed pie. Immigration makes a more innovative, flexible, and productive economy, leading to new and better jobs. The benefits rise over time, with an expanding economic pie.

Immigration also offers a mix of cultural benefits and challenges, complicated but manageable. Unfortunately, perverse government policies exacerbate political and sovereignty problems. For instance, affirmative action benefits immigrants whose ancestors suffered no discrimination. Bilingual education and foreign language ballots relieve pressure on immigrants to learn English. Welfare benefits and services attract putative dependents rather than incipient entrepreneurs.

While elites tend to favor increased immigration, the public is more hostile to opening America's borders. Indeed, immigration has become one of Washington's most emotional political battles, which makes it difficult to generate the political consensus necessary for change.

To move forward, Congress should separate employment from citizenship. Since the most obvious benefits of immigration are economic, legislators should expand work visas for multiple skill levels. Renewable permits should be issued to individuals; compliance could be enforced by requiring immigrants to post a bond or deposit some of their earnings in a bank account, payable upon their departure. Immigration auctions or tariffs also would be innovative alternatives.

The Status of Illegal Immigrants

Congress also should regularize the status of those currently in America illegally. Washington should grant residence and employment permits, renewable or permanent, to the undocumented, freeing them of the fear of deportation. They then would be more likely to invest in education and training and integrate into the larger surrounding community.

In contrast, Congress should leave debate over turning illegal aliens into fellow citizens as well as legal workers for the future. In fact, some policy makers are considering just such a compromise.

For instance, Rep. Raúl Labrador (R-ID) advocated "a legal process where people know they can be here for a long period of time, renew their visas, but you don't need a pathway to citizenship." The Republican National Committee [RNC] urged creation of renewable work permits without the promise of citizenship. Rep. Bob Goodlatte (R-VA), chairman of the House Judiciary Committee, asked: "Are there options that we should consider between the extremes of mass deportation and a pathway to citizenship?"

Some immigration critics complain that this approach would reward illegal behavior. The undocumented did break the law, but to improve their and their families' lives, not to hurt others. As President Barack Obama observed: "the vast majority of these individuals aren't looking for any trouble. They're just looking to provide for their families, contribute to their communities." Indeed, their presence benefits most Americans.

Moreover, there is no reason to expect that the 11 million people in America illegally will "self-deport." Most Americans don't have the stomach to round up millions of people who have become embedded in U.S. society. Additional employment controls and sanctions would undermine domestic liberties Americans take for granted. Regularization rather than deportation is the better choice.

The Controversy over Citizenship

Immigration supporters are even more critical of compromising on citizenship. After the RNC proposal, one blogger harkened back to the slave era, writing that the immigrants' "status would be akin to the freedman who were denied citizenship under the notorious Supreme Court decision in *Dred Scott* [referring to *Dred Scott v. Sandford*]." Cristina Jimenez of the youth organization United We Dream called the idea "un-American." Frank Sharry of America's Voice contended that the message to those allowed to work is that they "are not good enough to be one of us."

None of these charges make sense. In *Dred Scott* the court ruled that people who had been kidnapped, transported across the ocean, and forced to reside in America were not citizens, even after living in nominally "free" states. In contrast, today's undocumented came voluntarily without any expectation of becoming citizens. Moreover, they jumped the queue, leap-frogging those who were waiting, sometimes for years, to emigrate legally.

Certainly there is nothing "un-American" about not making those who came illegally citizens. There may be policy reasons for doing so. But a republic dedicated to the rule of law has no moral or political obligation to prefer those who violate legal process.

Nor does the issue involve being "good enough" to be a citizen. The world is filled with people who would be productive, creative, law-abiding, decent, and otherwise worthy American citizens. Not all of them can share in the benefits and responsibilities of American citizenship. Immigration policy requires making choices, imposing criteria, and establishing procedures. Those who come illegally have no greater claim to citizenship than anyone else.

Moreover, for immigrants seeking economic opportunity—which typifies the undocumented—legal residency and employment are more important than political participation. With the former two, they would enjoy most of the benefits of American society. Naturalization would result in some additional "rights," but regularization even without citizenship would dramatically improve the status of today's illegal immigrants.

Two Paths to a Legal Status

Indeed, many of those here illegally appear to prefer legality over citizenship. Only 40 percent of those eligible for citizenship under the 1986 legislation naturalized. Two-thirds of the 5.4 million Mexican immigrants eligible for citizenship have not done so.

Newly legalized residents who desired to become citizens could apply for citizenship under existing rules. Indeed, Rep. Goodlatte proposed granting illegal aliens provisional legal status, after which they could use existing law to apply for a green card and ultimately citizenship, but "none of those would be special ways that have been made available only to people who have come here illegally."

My Cato Institute colleague Alex Nowrasteh proposed creating two paths to permanent legal status, one a relatively simple process for gaining a work permit without an opportunity for citizenship, the other a more complex procedure allowing eventual citizenship. This, explained Nowrasteh, would "allow the unauthorized immigrants *themselves* to choose the type of legal status they wish to have," while allowing government to adjust requirements to meet policy ends.

Yet the editors of Bloomberg news complain that "legalization with no chance of citizenship would create an official second class." Others talk of a permanent "underclass." Actually, that's the case today. Legalizing the undocumented and improving their economic opportunities would empower them. They chose to come to America knowing they would be second class in every way—political, economic, and social. Regularizing their status would resolve the latter two issues.

161

A Question About Citizenship Policy

Every year, 300,000 to 400,000 children are born to illegal immigrants in the United States. Despite the foreign citizenship and illegal status of the parent, the executive branch of the U.S. government automatically recognizes these children as U.S. citizens upon birth. The same is true of children born to tourists and other aliens who are present in the United States in a legal but temporary status. Since large-scale tourism and mass illegal immigration are relatively recent phenomena, it is unclear for how long the U.S. government has followed this practice of automatic "birthright citizenship" without regard to the duration or legality of the mother's presence.

Eminent legal scholars and jurists . . . have questioned whether the 14th Amendment should be read to mandate such a permissive citizenship policy. Nevertheless, the practice has become the de facto law of the land without any input from Congress or the American public.

Advocates of maintaining this citizenship policy argue that the plain language of the citizenship clause of the 14th Amendment protects automatic birthright citizenship for all children born to illegal and temporary aliens. However, several legal scholars and political scientists who have delved into the history of the 14th Amendment have concluded that "subject to the jurisdiction thereof" has no plain meaning and that the executive branch's current, broad application of the citizenship clause may not be warranted.

John Feere, "Birthright Citizenship in the United States: A Global Comparison," Backgrounder, Center for Immigration Studies, August 2010.

The Free Movement of Labor

In fact, the newly legalized would resemble expatriate workers around the world. Foreign workers and residents make up about one-fifth of Switzerland's population. Often thought of as an insular society, Switzerland actually is cosmopolitan. It can freely welcome so many foreigners because it does not offer citizenship alongside employment.

The European Union [EU] allows free movement of labor throughout the continent unrelated to political rights. This process has become more controversial as the EU has expanded eastward to poorer states—Bulgaria and Romania, for instance. Nevertheless, concerns focus on competition with native workers, not development of a permanent underclass. Analyst Will Wilkinson cited the EU's "great practical and moral triumph: the dramatic expansion of European mobility rights and the inspiring integration of the continent's labor markets."

Several Persian Gulf states host numbers of foreign workers several times as large as native populations. This is not a great model for America—essentially Gulf citizens are on oil welfare and contract out most work to others. However, these nations capture the economic benefits of foreign workers without transforming their political systems, expanding their welfare programs, or creating underclass populations.

At the same time, those allowed to work but not rule are better off than those not allowed to work or rule. Some legal immigrants in America advocate this approach for those who came illegally. For instance, 24-year-old Mark Khazanovich, who emigrated from Russia with his family, told *The World* radio show: "If I was living in a terrible country, I would much rather have the option of living in America and not vote, than not live in America."

The Issue of Birthright Citizenship

Congress also should address the issue of "birthright" citizenship. The 14th Amendment proclaims: "All persons born or naturalized in the United States, and subject to the jurisdiction thereof, are citizens of the United States." Today everyone born in America, even to noncitizen parents merely visiting the U.S., become citizens.

The amendment was drafted to constitutionalize the citizenship of the freedmen after the Civil War, not set immigration policy. As Wilkinson explained, "Birthright citizenship made sense for a frontier country with open borders, newly freed slaves, and a small, remote bureaucracy. But the time seems ripe to consider alternatives."

There is no policy reason to automatically grant citizenship to the children of foreigners in America legally but with no significant connection to the country (such as tourists, businessmen, and diplomats) or to the children of those here illegally (irrespective of the latter's connection). The exact parameters of the constitutional mandate have not been established. Arguably those in America illegally are not subject to national jurisdiction, and therefore should not be covered. Congress should consider legislation or, if necessary, a constitutional amendment, to restrict birthright citizenship (for instance, to the children of those here legally) or eliminate it entirely.

America's simple test for citizenship offers obvious benefits, but only 33 of roughly 200 countries tie citizenship to birthplace. The only other developed nation to do so is Canada. Australia, France, Great Britain, Ireland, Malta, New Zealand, and Portugal all have abandoned birthright citizenship.

The Impact of Reform

Blogger Kevin Drum complained that changing citizenship rules would create "a large, permanent class of resentful noncitizens ... something nobody should be pining for." However, many of those granted birthright citizenship won't live in America as youths since their parents were merely visiting or temporarily stationed here.

Children of illegal immigrants usually stay, but they would benefit along with their parents from legalizing their status. Resentment is far more likely in response to impaired educational opportunities, poor job prospects, and arbitrary threats of deportation than to an inability to vote and run for office.

Blogger Timothy Lee worried that eliminating birthright citizenship would "permanently reduce the political clout of the immigrant community" and thereby hinder the cause of immigration reform. However, that's no argument for granting political rights to anyone born on American territory, irrespective of their parents' legal status or connection to America. Citizenship should be determined by more than temporary political convenience.

Of course, pushing legislation without citizenship and challenging birthright citizenship might cost political support from some reform advocates. Consultant Nicholas Montalto argued, "It will likely be impossible to reach a deal on comprehensive immigration reform with either the Senate or the House minority without such a well-defined path to citizenship." Sen. Marco Rubio (R-FL) said: "It must be clear from the outset that there is a pathway to citizenship." However, those advocating on behalf of the undocumented could not easily oppose a measure to legalize and empower the undocumented. Bloomberg's editors acknowledged that "legislation would be difficult for Democrats to resist" if a path for citizenship was provided for at least some currently illegal aliens.

Americans would greatly benefit from expanded immigration. However, enacting the right sort of reform remains politically difficult. Congress should allow more people to live and work legally in America, but put off the contentious argument over who should be welcomed as fellow citizens.

"Whatever the balance of total costs and
total benefits, disaggregation will reveal
that the beneficiaries of immigration
are very different from those who bear
its costs."

Not All Illegal Immigrants Should Be Treated the Same

Irwin M. Stelzer

*In the following viewpoint, Irwin M. Stelzer argues that current
immigration policy needs reform that avoids the errors of conflation and aggregation: All illegal immigrants are not deserving of
the same legal status and all immigrants do not offer the same
benefits to the United States. Stelzer contends that new policies
should reflect this while employing a mechanism for the beneficiaries of immigration to share the benefits with those adversely
affected by immigration. Stelzer is a senior fellow and director of
the Hudson Institute's economic policy studies group and a contributing editor of the* Weekly Standard.

Irwin M. Stelzer, "The Perils of Reform," *Weekly Standard*, vol. 18, no. 23, February 25,
2013. Copyright © 2013 The Weekly Standard. All rights reserved. Reprinted with permission.

As you read, consider the following questions:

1. Democrats garnered what fraction of the Latino vote in recent elections, according to Stelzer?

2. Rather than giving out work visas on the basis of family reunification, Stelzer suggests they be allocated in what way?

3. What fraction of the Service Employees International Union (SEIU) is Hispanic, according to the author?

Put vote-getting ahead of policy. Then conflate and aggregate. That's all you have to do to make a mess of immigration reform. Which is what our political class seems determined to do.

The Need for Immigration Reform

Although the details of reform legislation have yet to be worked out, the broad contours of the deal can be seen through the rhetorical haze that passes for political debate. Illegal immigrants will be granted probationary legal residence and the right to work if they have avoided any crimes other than crossing our border without permission. This amnesty will be followed by permanent residence, the first step on a path to citizenship, but only after a board of governors, state attorneys general, and notables from border states testify that the border has been secured. These probationary guests are to be denied access to Obamacare [referring to health care under the Patient Protection and Affordable Care Act] and other public assistance and will eventually have to pay back taxes when applying for citizenship.

There you have it. Sounds reasonable enough, with great appeal to the generosity of most Americans, many acquainted with some of these immigrants, whom they know to be hardworking. And to politicians in a bidding war for the votes of these citizens-to-be and, until then, of American citizens of Hispanic origin.

There is no denying that current policy needs fixing: As John McCain once told an insistent deport-them-all advocate at a small meeting in our living room, "Lady, we don't have 11 million pairs of handcuffs in America." Not only is mass deportation infeasible, it would be inhumane. More inhumane even than leaving 11 million people—12 million according to Patrick Leahy, chairman of the Senate Judiciary Committee, or is it 15 million as many of my Colorado neighbors contend?—to struggle along in some zone between illegality and de facto acceptance. As the president is fond of saying, "There is work to be done."

This is no easy chore. Emotions run high, not only among the illegal immigrants but among politicians who are in a bidding war for the favor of a voting bloc that is large and growing larger. So far, game, set, and match to the Democrats, who corralled some 70 percent of Latino voters in the recent elections, in part with promises of college and work permits for their kids—no legislation necessary, as the president exercised "prosecutorial discretion" on a massive scale. Now, a frightened batch of Republicans who once took a dim view of illegal border-crossing has entered the bidding in the hope of wooing this bloc to their banner.

Why they think this is possible is difficult to understand. Yes, many of these largely Hispanic illegal immigrants are socially conservative—they attend church, buy homes, start small businesses, and work hard, with over 90 percent of adult men in the labor market, according to Pia Orrenius and Madeline Zavodny, economists at the Dallas Fed [Federal Reserve Bank of Dallas] and Agnes Scott College, respectively. Those characteristics, argue conservative analysts in a display of the triumph of hope over experience, make them natural conservative voters. Alas, not so. There is another group that works hard, starts businesses, and should find the don't-overtax-the-rich mantra of Republicans attractive: Jews. But they identify with the underdog, even now, and see WASPy Republicans as less likely to understand them. Why Republicans think illegal immigrants, having trod the winding path to citizenship, will be any easier pickings than Jewish voters, I don't know. Surely, a better strategy than entering a bidding match against masters of that art would be to support sensible policies and compete for the great mass of voters on the basis of superior policy making rather than superior pandering.

The Error of Conflating Illegal Immigrants

That requires avoiding the twin perils of conflation and aggregation. Start with the error of conflating the need to do something about the status of illegals with providing them a path to citizenship. Many people who understand the desirability of giving these illegals some sort of stable life don't understand why that goal requires a path to citizenship for people who have jumped the queue. Granting legal status to these millions so that they might enjoy a more decent existence is one thing. Granting them the right to vote and to participate in the determination of the policies, domestic and foreign, of a nation they have entered illegally is quite another. Those who arrived as children, illegally but involuntarily, have a reasonable claim to more generous treatment. If recollection serves there is something in our tradition about not visiting the sins of the fathers on their sons. Arguably, creating a path to citizenship for this second generation is not a reward for illegal behavior, as it would be in the case of their parents. And, unlike their parents, this group will be proficient in the English language, as we define proficiency these days.

Their parents, however, have no claim that demands conflating the grant of a more secure status with citizenship. The British grant many people, this writer included, "indefinite leave to remain," which conveys the right of residence and freedom to find work, but not citizenship. Such a status might be a model for reform of our treatment of illegal immigrants. But do not for one moment believe that the millions with their residence "regularized" can be barred from the use of public services, a provision some would include in the immigration reform legislation. Teachers are not going to turn away such students, doctors are not going to refuse them care when they present themselves at hospitals in an emergency, police are not going to tell any who become crime victims that their assailants will not be pursued. Give them the right of residence, and you are effectively giving them access to the same public services to which citizens are entitled.

The Error of Aggregation

Having avoided the error of conflation, then disaggregate. The 11 million are not a homogeneous group. Everyone knows that; but the president and his party see their chances of getting the mass of the 11 million on the path to voterhood maximized by lumping millions of unskilled non-English speakers, nearly two-thirds of whom have never graduated from high school, with engineers who entered the country legally and received their advanced degrees here. That is why the president has warned Republicans "not to pull this thing apart," and the Democratic leadership in the Senate is insisting on a comprehensive bill—the sort preferred by [Democrat minority leader of the US House of Representatives] Nancy Pelosi, whose idea of good policy is not to find out what is in a bill until after you pass it.

Avoiding this politically inspired aggregation is one of the keys to sensible policy. A guest-worker program will take care of the needs of those who come for seasonal work: There is no need to issue permits that extend beyond the season or period in which those needs exist. Some will, of course, not go home and will overstay their visas. But far fewer than would were the amnesty granted the 11 million to include a path to citizenship. At the other end of the labor market, the highly trained and highly skilled can be granted both indefinite leave to remain and a path to citizenship, on the general theory that they will over their lifetimes provide a net benefit to the American economy and are more rather than less likely to learn English and otherwise assimilate. How many? Let employers bid for visas, rather than doling the bulk of them out for family reunification, and use the funds to offset some of the social costs imposed on communities with high percentages of immigrants.

After all, it is employer groups that are clamoring for more visas for these sorts of immigrants, whom they prefer to hire rather than the trained Americans available in ample supply, if data compiled by Ross Eisenbrey of the Economic Policy Institute [EPI] are to be believed. I have not attempted to decide whether the EPI data or the view of Caterpillar's chief technology officer Gwenne Henricks that we "need to have access to the best skills in higher volumes than we can access just out of the North American market" more closely represents reality. But even if Henricks is correct that such home-grown talents are not now available, it is unclear why increasing compensation for these skilled positions, rather than holding the line on pay by importing talent, would not increase the domestic supply in the long run. Which may be why the Silicon Valley CEOs [chief executive officers] are pressing so hard for comprehensive reform, without which "the odds of high-skilled [legislation] passing . . . is close to zero," according to Robert D. Atkinson, president of the Information Technology and Innovation Foundation.

Consider the analogy of the law business. When it was booming and compensation was rising, students flocked to law schools. Now that the bloom is off that rose, and law firms are either not hiring or keeping compensation under control, law school enrollment is plummeting, so much so that some schools are threatened with closure. The price system works, in labor markets as well as in the markets for goods and services.

The Policy for Existing Illegal Immigrants

Then there is the great mass of the illegals. These people should be allowed to stay, out of the shadows. In part because this is the humane thing to do, in part because we have no feasible way of deporting them, and in part because with few exceptions they are hardworking, granting the right to remain is worth the risk that it will encourage a new wave of illegal immigration. And that risk is far from trivial. After all, it would not be irrational for a prospective illegal entrant to believe that just as [Ronald] Reagan granted amnesty to 2.7 million in 1986, and we are now considering granting amnesty with a path to citizenship to 11 million, some day he or she will receive a similar blessing. Yes, the current amnesty is advertised as "probationary." But there is no conceivable circumstance under which the passage from probation to permanent residence to citizenship would be halted, unless the politicians in charge of determining whether the porosity of the border has been reduced declare that effort a failure. Anyone who believes that a group of vote-seeking politicians would risk antagonizing millions of potential voters might usefully spend his time bidding for a bridge in Brooklyn. And anyone who hopes that the Democrats among these judges will call a halt to the probationary millions' march to citizenship by declaring our borders insecure is doomed to disappointment.

After all, were it not for our tough job market and a miniboom in Mexico, the flow of immigration would not have receded in recent years. As Senator Marco Rubio pointed out in his response to last week's State of the Union address [in February 2013], the history of border controls is a history of "broken promises . . . to secure our borders and enforce our laws." Last week Chris Crane, president of the Immigration and Customs Enforcement agents' union, told a congressional committee, "We are under orders" not to enforce the law, and Michael Teitelbaum, former member of the Barbara Jordan Commission on Immigration Reform, has testified that there have been no "serious efforts" to control illegal immigration.

The Costs and Benefits of Immigration

This error of aggregation also applies to the cost-benefit studies that prove, or fail to prove, that immigration reform would be a net economic plus for the country as a whole. Whatever the balance of total costs and total benefits, disaggregation will reveal that the beneficiaries of immigration are very different from those who bear its costs.

Owners of large lawns and swimming pools quite naturally favor an increase in the supply of labor available to tend these suburban amenities; Americans who mow lawns, from schoolkids trying to earn a bit towards their education to grown-ups for whom these chores constitute a decent living if they can command a decent wage, are understandably less enthusiastic about this new, wage-lowering competition.

Labor union bureaucrats, who lust after the dues that come with new members, benefit from increasing the supply of legal workers who make beds and clean hotel rooms, as do vacationers and business travelers who might see room rates rise if hoteliers had to pay the wages that might prevail if the supply of workers were restricted to legal residents. American workers, including legal immigrants, who could do those jobs, or would do them if wages reflected the available supply of legal residents, bear the cost of the benefits that go to trade union leaders in the form of increased dues, to hoteliers in the form of higher profits, and to more affluent American business travelers and vacationers in the form of lower room rates. Little wonder that union leaders who want more dues payers oppose guest-worker programs that would legalize immigrants who come to work but plan (or say they plan) to return to their homeland when their work is completed. This itinerant group is notoriously difficult to unionize, whereas, once legalized, car washers and other such unskilled workers would join unions—one-fourth of the over two million members of the Service Employees International Union (SEIU) are Hispanic. "With papers, more of us will want to join the union," one of the 10,000, mostly illegal, Hispanic carwash workers in Los Angeles told the *Wall Street Journal*.

A Policy to Address the Mismatch

And the working-class Americans whose children are unchallenged in school owing to the large number of students who do not speak English pay a cost not borne by the Washington political class enthusiastically hunting for policies that will increase the flow of immigrants with still another amnesty, but whose kids attend [private Washington, DC, schools] Sidwell and St. Albans, and who live in school districts in which non-English-speaking students are only a minimal presence.

The mismatch between beneficiaries and those who bear the costs of immigration, ignored by policy makers but not by those who gain and those who lose, cries out for a mechanism by which the beneficiaries share those benefits with the millions of American households and workers adversely affected by immigration.

There you have it. Reform the broken immigration system. Allow the 11 million to "come out of the shadows," to use a phrase preferred by those who have not noticed that many even now enjoy the sunlight in welcoming cities and communities, but don't conflate that with a guaranteed path to citizenship. Set their more assimilable youngsters—innocent of intentional wrongdoing, and found by a Pew [Research Center] study to be at least as successful as the general population—on such a path. Then disaggregate. Legalize guest workers so employers cannot exploit them. Ease the path to permanent residence and citizenship for the highly educated and highly skilled, despite Obama's opposition to what the White House calls a "narrowly tailored proposal," with no explanation as to why such focused reforms are undesirable. Arrange for the beneficiaries of the new immigration policy to compensate those who will bear its costs. And by all means avoid one of those 2,000-page bills in which unseen evil lurks.

| "The United States should stop attempting to eliminate illegal immigrants—since that will never work—and focus instead on policies that treat them with humanity."

States Should Compete for Illegal Immigrants

Jagdish Bhagwati and Francisco Rivera-Batiz

In the following viewpoint, Jagdish Bhagwati and Francisco Rivera-Batiz argue that new federal legislation will not stop the flow of illegal immigrants and that stricter border enforcement has only led to inhumane treatment of illegal immigrants. They argue that states should compete for illegal immigrants through more humane laws that advance human rights. Bhagwati is a professor at Columbia University and a senior fellow for international economics at the Council on Foreign Relations. Rivera-Batiz is a professor of economics and education at the Teachers College, Columbia University.

As you read, consider the following questions:

1. According to the authors, the 1986 Immigration Reform and Control Act was based on what failed assumption?

2. The authors draw an analogy with what historical event to bolster their claim that it is not possible to stop the flow of illegal immigrants?

3. Which five states do the authors identify as hostile to illegal immigrants and which four as more welcoming?

E ver since Congress passed the Immigration Reform and Control Act, in 1986, attempts at a similar comprehensive reform of U.S. immigration policies have failed. Yet today, as the Republican Party smarts from its poor performance among Hispanic voters in 2012 and such influential Republicans as former Florida governor Jeb Bush have come out in favor of a new approach, the day for comprehensive immigration reform may seem close at hand. President Barack Obama was so confident about its prospects that he asked for it in his State of the Union address in February 2013. Now, the U.S. Senate looks poised to offer illegal immigrants a pathway to citizenship.

But a top-down legislative approach to immigration could nonetheless easily die in Congress, just as the last serious one did, in 2007. Indeed, the president's domestic problems with health care and foreign problems with Syria have already cast a shadow over the prospects for reform.

The Challenges to Eliminating Illegal Immigration

Even if a bill did manage to pass, the sad fact is that it would work no better than the 1986 law did. That act was based on the assumption that punishments, such as sanctions on employers and heightened border security, and incentives, such as an increase in the number of legal immigrants allowed to enter the country and amnesty for illegal immigrants already there, could eliminate illegal immigration altogether. That assumption proved illusory: The offer of amnesty may have temporarily reduced the stock of illegal immigrants, but it was not enough to eliminate it. Nor did employer sanctions and border enforcement reduce the flow of new illegal immigrants.

The challenges to eliminating illegal immigration are, if anything, greater today than they were in 1986. For one thing, in order to make today's proposals politically feasible, their authors decided to offer illegal immigrants not immediate unconditional amnesty but a protracted process of legalization. Confronted with this approach, a large share of the estimated 11 million illegal immigrants now living in the United States would likely choose to remain illegal rather than gamble on the distant promise of naturalization.

Nor would reform dissuade new illegal immigrants from joining those already in the country. Extrapolating from the recent drop in apprehensions near the Rio Grande [a river that flows from Colorado to the Gulf of Mexico], some analysts have argued that since the flow of illegal immigrants has already slowed to a trickle, the issue has lost its urgency. This notion is misguided. One cannot focus just on the area around the Rio Grande, since only half of all illegal immigrants residing in the United States entered the country by unlawfully crossing the U.S.-Mexican border, according to a 2006 study by the Pew Research Center. Moreover, whatever drop-off has occurred is mostly the result of the recent economic slowdown in the United States and will not prove permanent. As long as wages in the United States greatly outstrip those in poor countries, the United States will remain a mecca for potential immigrants, legal and illegal.

Not only would immigration reform fail to achieve its goal of eliminating illegal immigrants; it would also lead to increasingly draconian treatment of them. In order to appease anti-immigrant groups, the Senate's immigration reform bill provides for stricter enforcement of the U.S.-Mexican border, along with $40 billion in funding. But past experience suggests that such regulations are an exercise in futility: They do little to slow the influx of illegal immigrants while greatly increasing the risk to their lives as they try to cross the border over more dangerous terrain, aided by unscrupulous smugglers who may abandon them mid-journey.

Given these realities, the United States should stop attempting to eliminate illegal immigrants—since that will never work—and focus instead on policies that treat them with humanity. Doing so would mean adopting a variety of measures to diminish the public's hostility to illegal immigrants. Principal among them would be a shift from a top-down approach to a bottom-up one: letting states compete for illegal immigrants. States with laws that were unfriendly to illegal immigrants would lose them and their badly needed labor to states that were more welcoming. The result would be a competition that would do far more to improve the treatment of illegal immigrants than anything coming from Washington.

The Difficulties with Compromise

Americans can be schizophrenic when it comes to illegal immigration, suffering from a sort of right-brain, left-brain problem. The right brain sympathizes with illegal immigrants, since they are immigrants, after all, and the United States was founded on immigration. But the left brain fixates on their illegality, which offends Americans' respect for the rule of law. Negotiating a viable compromise between those who wish to throw illegal immigrants out and those who wish to embrace them has always proved exceptionally difficult. As the historian Mae Ngai has shown, U.S. immigration policy in the 1920s and 1930s was as conflicted as it is today, with proponents of deportations pitted against pro-immigrant humanitarian groups.

Further complicating matters is Americans' sense of fairness. Liberals have called on Congress to offer illegal immigrants a path to citizenship, but unlike most other countries, the United States has an enormous backlog of potential immigrants who have dutifully lined up for entry—an issue that Spain, for example, did not face when it granted its illegal immigrants amnesty in 2005. Many Americans consider it unfair to let immigrants who have broken the law join the same line that those who followed the rules are in. The proponents of amnesty have, in consequence, cluttered up their proposed policy with various restrictions and requirements that make it far less attractive than a forthright granting of full citizenship.

Like past reform proposals, the current one offers illegal immigrants a long road to legality. But the longer the process, the greater the risk that a new Congress will reverse the old. Many illegal immigrants may prefer not to accept that risk and instead stay illegal. Furthermore, as the immigration scholars Mark Rosenzweig, Guillermina Jasso, Douglas Massey, and James Smith have shown, around 30 percent of U.S. immigrants achieve legal status despite having violating immigration laws in the past. Taking these factors into account, it is reasonable to predict that of the estimated 11 million illegal immigrants, only half would take an offer of amnesty, perhaps less.

The Illusion of Ending Illegal Immigration

Just like the chimera of legalizing away the stock of illegal immigrants, the notion that the flow of new illegal immigrants can be shut off is also deeply impractical. For instance, attempts at expanding legal immigration in the hope that it will reduce the incentive for illegal immigration would require, at minimum, vastly expanded legal admissions. Yet even though trade unions have given up their long-standing opposition to legalizing illegal immigrants—which they figure will boost their membership—they oppose significantly expanding legal

Frank and Ernest

THIS IS NOT WHAT I MEANT BY "HUDDLED MASSES".

JULY IV

© Thaves/Cartoonist Group.

admissions. Unions have long blamed immigration for the stagnation of workers' wages, just as they have blamed outsourcing and trade liberalization. In fact, the AFL-CIO [American Federation of Labor and Congress of Industrial Organizations] recently suggested that it should be involved in determining how many legal guest workers the United States will admit in the future. When President George W. Bush proposed a more expansive guest-worker program, unions helped kill the measure, and they would fiercely fight any efforts to liberalize legal immigration this time, too.

It is also dubious that draconian enforcement measures, at the border or internally, would actually intimidate would-be illegal immigrants, no matter what mix of punishments and inducements Congress legislates. Unlike in 1986, almost every U.S. immigrant is now more secure: Their ethnic compatriots will, as they already do, go to bat for better treatment, raising their voices against such measures.

But the biggest hurdle that immigration reform faces is that as long as immigration restrictions exist, people will continue to enter the United States illegally. The government can send as many Eliot Nesses to Chicago to nab as many Al Capones as it wants, but the bootlegged liquor will keep flowing across the Canadian border as long as Prohibition remains in place.

The Impact of Stricter Border Enforcement

Short of dismantling all border restrictions, then, no policy could magically eliminate illegal immigration. Yet not only would a reform bill be ineffective; it could also be harmful. If a comprehensive reform bill were passed, there is a serious danger that policy makers, operating on the flawed assumption that there should then be no reason for illegal immigrants to exist, might enact even harsher measures against them.

In fact, merely attempting to secure support for a reform bill is certain to harm illegal immigrants. Their experiences under President Bill Clinton and Obama have not been reassuring. Although Democrats have generally been more sympathetic to illegal immigrants than have Republicans, both Clinton and Obama, in their attempts to secure bipartisan consensus on immigration reform, implemented ruthless measures against illegal immigrants.

In the wake of the Immigration Reform and Control Act, the U.S. government ramped up enforcement at the border, which reached new heights during the Clinton administration. Ditches were built and fences constructed. To seal off common routes of entry into the United States, the government mounted military-style actions with names that seemed straight out of a war room: Operation Blockade, in El Paso in 1993; Operation Gatekeeper, in San Diego in 1994; and many more. The border security budget skyrocketed, rising from $326 million in 1992 to $1.1 billion by the time President George W. Bush took office, in 2001. The number of U.S. Border Patrol agents stationed at the southwestern border nearly tripled. In the end, these measures did little to stem the inflow. The demographer Jeffrey Passel of the Pew Research

Center has estimated that the average net annual influx of illegal immigrants crossing the Rio Grande rose from 324,000 in the first half of the 1990s to 654,800 in the second half of the decade.

What stricter enforcement did do was force illegal immigrants to bypass safer crossing points and travel through the desert instead. Desperate immigrants made no secret of their desire to keep trying to sneak across the border despite heightened enforcement, often attempting again and again until they got through. But crossing the desert meant that they had to pay smugglers, known as coyotes, who left carloads of illegal immigrants for dead when they feared apprehension by U.S. Border Patrol personnel. At best, the Clinton administration's policies had a marginal impact on illegal border traffic and led to a major decline in the welfare of those trying to enter the country illegally. They also failed to achieve their larger objective of getting legislation through Congress; the "keep them out" and "throw them out" lobbies were too strongly opposed to any compromise.

Obama has ramped up border enforcement, too, but he has also deported record numbers of illegal immigrants already living in the United States. In 2011, he expanded the Secure Communities initiative, a joint effort between state and local governments—the federal authorities have even ordered uncooperative states, such as New York, to fall in line—that uses integrated databases to track down illegal immigrants. According to official statistics, the number of deportations (excluding apprehensions at the border itself) has risen under Obama, to 395,000 in 2009. In 2001, under George W. Bush, deportations numbered only 189,000.

The Need to Shift Focus

The focus on border enforcement is misguided. In part, it owes to the false equation of lax border control with the influx of terrorists. There is little evidence of that link: even the

9/11 [referring to the September 11, 2001, terrorist attacks on the United States] hijackers entered the United States legally. Moreover, correcting for the effect of the recession on attempted crossings, it is clear that the impact of Obama's policies has been far from dramatic in deterring illegal immigration. But the distress caused to illegal immigrants has been great. As a 2011 report from Human Rights Watch detailed, tens of thousands of immigrants are shuffled from jail to jail awaiting deportation. Once again, the country has gained little and lost much.

With top-down immigration reform unworkable and inhumane, Americans need to shift their focus to treating their inevitable neighbors with humanity. That objective cannot be pursued through Washington. It must come from elsewhere: competition among states. States that harass illegal immigrants, such as Alabama, Arizona, Georgia, Indiana, and South Carolina, will drive illegal immigrants to more welcoming states, such as Maryland, New York, Utah, and Washington. As the former lose badly needed cheap labor to the latter, the political equilibrium will shift toward those who favor policies that help retain and attract illegal immigrants.

Of course, states cannot intrude on the parts of immigration enforcement over which the federal government has exclusive authority, such as border control and civil rights. But there are a number of steps states can take to make life easier for illegal immigrants, such as issuing them driver's licenses and making accessible to them everything from health care to university scholarships.

The Impact of Fleeing Illegal Immigrants

Illegal immigrants are already voting with their feet, leaving or bypassing states that treat them harshly and flocking to those with more benign policies. In 2011, hours after a federal judge in Alabama upheld most of the state's strict immigration law, illegal immigrants began fleeing. Frightened families, the *New York Times* reported, "left behind mobile homes, sold fully furnished for a thousand dollars or even less." The article continued: "Two, 5, 10 years of living here, and then gone in a matter of days, to Tennessee, Illinois, Oregon, Florida, Arkansas, Mexico—who knows? Anywhere but Alabama."

Ample statistical evidence demonstrates this pattern. From 1990 to 2010, when tough border-enforcement policies (which naturally focused on the border states) were in vogue, Arizona, California, New Mexico, and Texas saw their collective share of illegal immigrants decline by 17 percent. In California alone, the percentage of all illegal immigrants residing there fell from 43 percent to 23 percent. Similarly, the economists Sarah Bohn, Magnus Lofstrom, and Steven Raphael have calculated that Arizona's 2007 Legal Arizona Workers Act, which banned businesses from hiring illegal immigrants, led to a notable decline in the proportion of the state's foreign-born Hispanic population.

The resulting blow to economic activity has often been drastic; employers in agriculture and construction, for example, regularly complain about the absence of workers. Fortunately, however, as business interests begin to agitate in favor of easing up on illegal immigrants, state capitals will start taking note. Already, many groups in the unwelcoming states have begun to question their states' draconian immigration enforcement laws and argue for more modest measures. After Alabama passed its immigration law, for example, business leaders complained to lawmakers about the resulting labor shortages. After the Legal Arizona Workers Act went into effect, in 2008, the state's contractors' trade association even joined civil rights groups in seeking the law's repeal. That same year, the U.S. Chamber of Commerce filed a lawsuit challenging the constitutionality of an Oklahoma law that required employers to verify the work status of their employees.

The Need for a Race to the Top

As this dynamic plays out, states will begin to compete for illegal immigrants, who will then face less harassment and be able to better integrate into their communities. Democrats and Republicans who care about human rights should welcome this change. More important, so should Republicans who prize states' rights. A race to the top in the treatment of illegal immigrants is a viable path to reform that would greatly advance human rights in the United States.

There are other ways to improve the lives of illegal immigrants that also do not involve Washington. Consider the problem of Mexicans who risk their lives traveling through the desert while attempting to cross the border and who occasionally damage the property of Texan ranchers. With no method to recoup their losses, the affected ranchers found it tempting to join forces with the Minutemen vigilantes who used to patrol the border. To reduce ranchers' hostility toward illegal immigrants, the Mexican government should set up a fund that compensates ranchers who can establish credible claims of damage. Since the stories of such damages tend to outstrip the reality, the fund need not be particularly large to go a long way in defusing the hostility.

Another way to improve the plight of illegal immigrants would be for Mexico to help pay for the education and medical expenses of those illegal immigrants coming from Mexico that are otherwise borne by the U.S. government. Although a number of studies show that illegal immigrants represent a net contribution to U.S. government coffers, the common perception that American taxpayers must bear these costs and that Mexico should share some of the burden of its own citizens breeds resentment. Were the Mexican government to make such a contribution, it would serve as a gesture of goodwill that could help reduce the hostility toward illegal immigrants.

"Give me your tired, your poor, your huddled masses," reads the poem by Emma Lazarus that adorns the Statue of Liberty, which once welcomed the millions of immigrants arriving at Ellis Island. It is well past time to revive that sense of humanity, and the diverse recommendations outlined here can help the United States do just that. Whether or not they come with Washington's permission, immigrants to the United States nonetheless deserve the compassion Lazarus promised.

Periodical and Internet Sources Bibliography

The following articles have been selected to supplement the diverse views presented in this chapter.

Ronald Brownstein	"Why the Time Is Finally Right for 'Amnesty,'" *National Journal*, April 18, 2013.
Marshall Fitz	"Piecemeal Immigration Proposals Miss the Point: A Path to Citizenship Is a Political and Policy Imperative," Center for American Progress, December 11, 2012.
Conor Friedersdorf	"The Thorny Issue of Illegal Immigration and the Rule of Law," *Atlantic*, August 5, 2011.
William P. Hoar	"Lawmakers Advocate Amnesty for 11 Million Lawbreakers," *New American*, June 3, 2013.
Robert Lynch and Patrick Oakford	"The Economic Effects of Granting Legal Status and Citizenship to Undocumented Immigrants," Center for American Progress, March 20, 2013.
Warren Mass	"Permanent Amnesty, Temporary Border," *New American*, April 8, 2013.
Pia M. Orrenius and Madeline Zavodny	"The Economic Consequences of Amnesty for Unauthorized Immigrants," *Cato Journal*, vol. 32, no. 1, Winter 2012.
Laura Pereyra	"The High Price of Immigration Enforcement Without Immigration Reform," *National Journal*, August 30, 2012.
Sierra Rayne	"Discretionary Illegal Immigration Is Bad Policy," *American Thinker*, September 14, 2013.
Greg Sargent	"How to Know Whether GOP Is Serious About Immigration Reform," *Washington Post*, January 27, 2014.

For Further Discussion

Chapter 1

1. Eric Posner and Victor Davis Hanson both talk about who benefits from illegal immigration. What areas are they in agreement? Disagreement? Cite examples from the viewpoints to support your answer.

2. Both Daniel Griswold and Adam Davidson point to research that supports the view that immigration overall (legal and illegal) benefits the economy. Does this prove that *illegal* immigration is an overall benefit? Why, or why not?

3. How does Steve Chapman explain away the federal crime statistics on illegal immigrants raised by the Federation for American Immigration Reform (FAIR)?

Chapter 2

1. The Heritage Foundation Immigration and Border Security Reform Task Force argues that the US-Mexican border needs increased security to reduce illegal immigration to the United States. What are some of the measures the task force suggests? Do you think implementing such measures will reduce illegal immigration? Explain, citing examples from the viewpoint to support your reasoning.

2. Gabriel Arana claims that it is impossible to completely seal the borders. Is this, by itself, a reason against greater border enforcement? Why, or why not? Draw on at least one of the other authors in this chapter to justify your answer.

Chapter 3

1. Cory Gardner, Ira Mehlman, and Jeff Denham provide competing arguments regarding what to do about the sta-

tus of illegal immigrants brought to the United States as children. Who do you think has the best proposal, and why?

2. Keegan Hamilton questions why President Barack Obama doesn't just halt the deportations of all noncriminal undocumented immigrants. How might Mark Krikorian argue that there is no such class of illegal immigrants?

3. Charles Garcia and Jon Feere debate the language used to describe those who remain in the United States illegally. Does the language here run the risk of begging the question? Is any terminology completely neutral? Explain.

Chapter 4

1. Marshall Fitz says undocumented immigrants are "already Americans in everything but paperwork." How do you think Mark Krikorian would respond to this claim?

2. Irwin M. Stelzer suggests businesses bid for work visas for immigrant workers, whereas Jagdish Bhagwati and Francisco Rivera-Batiz suggest that states compete for illegal immigrants. How do you think the other authors in this chapter would react to these suggestions? Discuss the views of at least two other authors in relation to one or both of these suggestions.

Organizations to Contact

The editors have compiled the following list of organizations concerned with the issues debated in this book. The descriptions are derived from materials provided by the organizations. All have publications or information available for interested readers. The list was compiled on the date of publication of the present volume; the information provided here may change. Be aware that many organizations take several weeks or longer to respond to inquiries, so allow as much time as possible.

American Civil Liberties Union (ACLU)
125 Broad Street, 18th Floor, New York, NY 10004
(212) 549-2500
e-mail: infoaclu@aclu.org
website: www.aclu.org

The American Civil Liberties Union (ACLU) is a national organization that works to defend Americans' civil rights as guaranteed in the US Constitution. The ACLU's Immigrants' Rights Project is dedicated to expanding and enforcing the civil liberties and civil rights of noncitizens as well as combating public and private discrimination against immigrants. The ACLU publishes the semiannual newsletter *Civil Liberties Alert* as well as briefing papers, including the publication "What ICE Isn't Telling You About Detainers."

American Immigration Control (AIC) Foundation
PO Box 525, Monterey, VA 24465
(540) 468-2023 • fax: (540) 468-2026
website: www.aicfoundation.com

The American Immigration Control (AIC) Foundation is a nonpartisan organization that favors deportation of illegal immigrants and opposes amnesty and guest-worker legislation. The foundation works to inform American citizens on the disastrous effects of uncontrolled immigration. It publishes several books, videos, and reports on the topic of immigration, including the policy brief "How Immigration Drove California's Decline."

American Immigration Council

1331 G Street NW, Suite 200, Washington, DC   20005
(202) 507-7500
website: www.americanimmigrationcouncil.org

The American Immigration Council is an educational organization that works to strengthen America by honoring its immigrant history. The council promotes humane immigration policies that honor human rights and works to achieve fairness for immigrants under the law. It publishes numerous fact sheets and reports through its Immigration Policy Center, including "The Growth of the US Deportation Machine."

Center for American Progress

1333 H Street NW, 10th Floor, Washington, DC   20005
(202) 682-1611
website: www.americanprogress.org

The Center for American Progress is a nonprofit, nonpartisan organization dedicated to improving the lives of Americans through progressive ideas and action. The center dialogues with leaders, thinkers, and citizens to explore the vital issues facing America and the world. The Center for American Progress publishes numerous research papers, which are available at its website, including "The Economic Case for a Clear, Quick Pathway to Citizenship."

Center for Immigration Studies

1629 K Street NW, Suite 600, Washington, DC   20006
(202) 466-8185 • fax: (202) 466-8076
website: www.cis.org

The Center for Immigration Studies is an independent research organization dedicated to providing immigration policy makers, the academic community, news media, and concerned citizens with reliable information about the social, economic, environmental, security, and fiscal consequences of legal and illegal immigration into the United States. The center is animated by a unique "low-immigration, pro-immigrant" vision that seeks fewer immigrants but a warmer welcome for those admitted. The center publishes reports, memos, and opinion pieces, including "Asylum in the United States."

Federation for American Immigration Reform (FAIR)
25 Massachusetts Avenue NW, Suite 330
Washington, DC   20001
(877) 627-3247
website: www.fairus.org

The Federation for American Immigration Reform (FAIR) is a nonprofit organization of concerned citizens who share a common belief that the nation's immigration policies must be reformed to serve the national interest. FAIR seeks to improve border security, to stop illegal immigration, and to promote immigration levels at rates of about three hundred thousand a year. FAIR publishes the monthly *Immigration Report* and other publications, including "Illegal Aliens Taking US Jobs."

Migration Policy Institute (MPI)
1400 Sixteenth Street NW, Suite 300, Washington, DC   20036
(202) 266-1940 • fax: (202) 266-1900
e-mail: info@migrationpolicy.org
website: www.migrationpolicy.org

The Migration Policy Institute (MPI) is an independent, nonpartisan think tank dedicated to analysis of the movement of people worldwide. MPI provides analysis, development, and evaluation of migration and refugee policies at the local, national, and international levels. MPI publishes books, reports, and fact sheets, including "Major US Immigration Laws, 1790–Present."

National Council of La Raza (NCLR)
1126 Sixteenth Street NW, Suite 600, Washington, DC   20036

(202) 785-1670 • fax: (202) 776-1792
e-mail: comments@nclr.org
website: www.nclr.org

The National Council of La Raza (NCLR) is a national organization that promotes civil rights and aims to improve opportunities for Hispanics. NCLR conducts applied research, policy analysis, and advocacy, providing a Latino perspective in five key areas, including immigration. NCLR publishes reports and issue briefs, including "The Impact of Section 287(g) of the Immigration and Nationality Act on the Latino Community."

National Immigration Forum
50 F Street NW, Suite 300, Washington, DC   20001
(202) 347-0040 • fax: (202) 347-0058
e-mail: info@immigrationforum.org
website: www.immigrationforum.org

The National Immigration Forum is an organization that advocates for the value of immigrants and immigration to the nation. The forum works to advance sound federal immigration solutions through policy expertise, communications outreach, and coalition-building work. It publishes numerous backgrounders, fact sheets, and issue papers, including "The Importance of Citizenship."

National Immigration Law Center (NILC)
3435 Wilshire Boulevard, Suite 2850, Los Angeles, CA   90010
(213) 639-3900 • fax: (213) 639-3911
website: www.nilc.org

The National Immigration Law Center (NILC) is dedicated to protecting and promoting the rights of low-income immigrants and their family members. NILC engages in policy advocacy, impact litigation, and education to secure fair treatment in the courts for immigrants, preserve a safety net for immigrants, and provide opportunities for immigrants. NILC publishes manuals and analyses for nonprofit agencies working on immigration issues, including *Immigrants' Rights Update*, a newsletter focused on changes in policy, legislation, and case law affecting low-income immigrants.

National Network for Immigrant and Refugee Rights (NNIRR)

310 Eighth Street, Suite 303, Oakland, CA   94607
(510) 465-1984 • fax: (510) 465-1885
e-mail: nnirrinfo@nnirr.org
website: www.nnirr.org

The National Network for Immigrant and Refugee Rights (NNIRR) is a national organization made up of local coalitions as well as immigrant, refugee, community, religious, civil rights, and labor organizations and activists. NNIRR works to promote a just immigration and refugee policy in the United States and to defend and expand the rights of all immigrants and refugees, regardless of immigration status. NNIRR publishes fact sheets and reports, including "Immigration Trends Overview."

Negative Population Growth (NPG)

2861 Duke Street, Suite 36, Alexandria, VA   22314
(703) 370-9510 • fax: (703) 370-9514
website: www.npg.org

Negative Population Growth (NPG) is an organization that aims to educate the American public and political leaders about the detrimental effects of overpopulation on the environment, resources, and quality of life. NPG advocates a smaller US population accomplished through reduced legal immigration rates and smaller families. NPG publishes a quarterly newsletter, *Population Perspectives*; a bimonthly journal, *NPG Journal*; and numerous forum papers, including "Hurtling Toward 50 Million: California Expands the Welcome Mat for Illegal Immigration."

US Citizenship and Immigration Services (USCIS)

425 I Street NW, Washington, DC   20536

(800) 375-5283
website: www.uscis.gov

US Citizenship and Immigration Services (USCIS) is the government agency that oversees lawful immigration to the United States. USCIS provides immigration information, grants immigration and citizenship benefits, promotes an awareness and understanding of citizenship, and ensures the integrity of the US immigration system. USCIS provides numerous reports and publishes a blog, *The Beacon*, with articles such as "A Nation of Laws and a Nation of Immigrants."

US Immigration and Customs Enforcement (ICE)
500 Twelfth Street SW, Washington, DC   20536
website: www.ice.gov

US Immigration and Customs Enforcement (ICE) is the principal investigative arm of the US Department of Homeland Security (DHS). ICE's primary mission is to promote homeland security and public safety through the criminal and civil enforcement of federal laws governing border control, customs, trade, and immigration. ICE publishes the quarterly *Cornerstone Report*, fact sheets, and reports.

Bibliography of Books

Darrell Ankarlo — *Illegals: The Unacceptable Cost of America's Failure to Control Its Borders*. Nashville, TN: Thomas Nelson, 2010.

Deborah A. Boehm — *Intimate Migrations: Gender, Family, and Illegality Among Transnational Mexicans*. New York: New York University Press, 2012.

Joseph H. Carens — *The Ethics of Immigration*. New York: Oxford University Press, 2013.

Joseph H. Carens — *Immigrants and the Right to Stay*. Cambridge, MA: MIT Press, 2010.

Maria Chávez, Jessica L. Lavariega Monforti, and Melissa R. Michelson — *Living the Dream: New Immigration Policies and the Lives of Undocumented Latino Youth*. Boulder, CO: Paradigm Publishers, 2014.

Aviva Chomsky — *Undocumented: How Immigration Became Illegal*. Boston, MA: Beacon Press, 2014.

William R. Daniel — *One If by Land: What Every American Needs to Know About Our Border*. Tucson, AZ: Wheatmark, 2012.

D. Robert DeChaine, ed. — *Border Rhetorics: Citizenship and Identity on the US-Mexico Frontier*. Tuscaloosa: University of Alabama Press, 2012.

Peter Eichstaedt   *The Dangerous Divide: Peril and
                        Promise on the US-Mexico Border.*
                        Chicago, IL: Lawrence Hill Books,
                        2014.

Tanya   *Due Process Denied: Detentions and
Golash-Boza   Deportations in the United States.*
                        New York: Routledge, 2012.

Alfonso Gonzales   *Reform Without Justice: Latino
                        Migrant Politics and the Homeland
                        Security State.* New York: Oxford
                        University Press, 2014.

John M. Gosselin,   *Immigration and Electronic
ed.   Employment Eligibility Verification.*
                        New York: Nova Science Publishers,
                        2013.

Jeremy Harding   *Border Vigils: Keeping Migrants Out of
                        the Rich World.* New York: Verso,
                        2012.

Samantha   *The Criminalization of Immigration:
Hauptman   The Post 9/11 Moral Panic.* El Paso,
                        TX: LFB Scholarly Publishing LLC,
                        2013.

Kelly Lytle   *Migra!: A History of the U.S. Border
Hernández   Patrol.* Berkeley: University of
                        California Press, 2010.

Janey Levy   *Illegal Immigration and Amnesty:
                        Open Borders and National Security.*
                        New York: Rosen Publishing, 2010.

Taylor M. Lindall,   *Border Security and the Removal of
ed.   Illegal Aliens.* New York: Nova Science
                        Publishers, 2011.

Sylvia Longmire   *Border Insecurity: Why Big Money,*
                   Fences, and Drones Aren't Making Us
                   Safer. New York: Palgrave Macmillan,
                   2014.

Eithne Luibhéid   *Pregnant on Arrival: Making the*
                   Illegal Immigrant. Minneapolis:
                   University of Minnesota Press, 2013.

Pilar Marrero   *Killing the American Dream: How*
                   Anti-Immigration Extremists Are
                   Destroying the Nation. New York:
                   Palgrave Macmillan, 2012.

Anne McNevin   *Contesting Citizenship: Irregular*
                   Migrants and the New Frontiers of the
                   Political. New York: Columbia
                   University Press, 2011.

Deirdre M.   *National Insecurities: Immigrants and*
Moloney   *U.S. Deportation Policy Since 1882.*
                   Chapel Hill: University of North
                   Carolina Press, 2012.

Mae M. Ngai   *Impossible Subjects: Illegal Aliens and*
                   the Making of Modern America.
                   Princeton, NJ: Princeton University
                   Press, 2014.

Peter Schrag   *Not Fit for Our Society: Immigration*
                   and Nativism in America. Berkeley:
                   University of California Press, 2010.

Harel Shapira   *Waiting for José: The Minutemen's*
                   Pursuit of America. Princeton, NJ:
                   Princeton University Press, 2013.

Rogers M. Smith, ed.	*Citizenship, Borders, and Human Needs.* Philadelphia: University of Pennsylvania Press, 2011.
Terry Greene Sterling	*Illegal: Life and Death in Arizona's Immigration War Zone.* Guilford, CT: Lyons Press, 2010.
Richard M. Taylor and Louis O. Walker, eds.	*Border Security and Illegal Immigration Enforcement.* New York: Nova Science Publishers, 2012.
Daniel M. Turcotte, ed.	*U.S. Immigration: Key Trends, Policies and Programs.* New York: Nova Science Publishers, 2013.

Index